Presidents house, Washington City, Nov. 2. 1800

My dearest friend

       We arrived here last night, or rather yesterday at one O Clock, and here we dined and Slept. The Building is in a State to be habitable. And now we wish for your Company. The Account you give of the melancholly State of our dear Brother Mr Cranch and his family is really distressing and must Severely afflict you, I most cordially Sympathize with you and them.

       I have Seen only Mr Marshall and Mr Stoddert General Wilkinson and the two Commissioners Mr Scott and Mr Thornton.

       I Shall Say nothing of public affairs. I am very glad you consented to come on, for you would have been more anxious at Quincy than here, and I, to all my other Solicitudines Mordaces as Horace calls them i.e. "Biting Cares" Should have added a great deal on your Account. Besides it is fit and proper that you and I Should retire together and not one before the other

Before I end my Letter I pray Heaven to bestow the best of Blessings on this House and all that shall hereafter inhabit it. May none but honest and wise Men ever rule under this roof.

I shall not attempt a description of it. You will form the best Idea of it from Inspection.

Mr Brisler is very anxious for the arrival of the Man and Women and I am much more so for that of the Ladies. I am with unabated confi- dence and affection yours

John Adams

ALSO BY DAVID McCULLOUGH

The Wright Brothers

The Greater Journey

1776

John Adams

Truman

Brave Companions

Mornings on Horseback

The Path Between the Seas

The Great Bridge

The Johnstown Flood

The
AMERICAN
SPIRIT

WHO WE ARE
and
WHAT WE STAND FOR

Speeches by

DAVID
McCULLOUGH

Simon & Schuster Paperbacks

New York   London   Toronto   Sydney   New Delhi

Simon & Schuster Paperbacks
An Imprint of Simon & Schuster, Inc.
1230 Avenue of the Americas
New York, NY 10020

"Simon Willard's Clock" originally appeared in *Brave Companions* by David McCullough in 1992 (Simon & Schuster).

"Power and the Presidency: What's Essential Is Invisible" originally appeared in *Power and the Presidency* edited by Robert A. Wilson in 1999 (PublicAffairs).

First Simon & Schuster paperback edition April 2018

SIMON & SCHUSTER PAPERBACKS and colophon are registered trademarks of Simon & Schuster, Inc.

For information about special discounts for bulk purchases, please contact Simon & Schuster Special Sales at 1-866-506-1949 or business@simonandschuster.com.

The Simon & Schuster Speakers Bureau can bring authors to your live event. For more information or to book an event contact the Simon & Schuster Speakers Bureau at 1-866-248-3049 or visit our website at www.simonspeakers.com.

Interior design by Joy O'Meara

Manufactured in the United States of America

10 9 8 7 6 5 4 3 2 1

The Library of Congress has cataloged the hardcover edition as follows:

Names: McCullough, David G., author.
Title: The American spirit : who we are and what we stand for / speeches by David McCullough.
Description: First Simon & Schuster hardcover edition. | New York : Simon & Schuster, 2017
Identifiers: LCSH 2017002640 | ISBN 9781501174216 | ISBN 1501174215 | ISBN 9781501174209 (ebook)
Subjects: LCSH: McCullough, David G.—Oratory. | National characteristics, American. | United States—Civilization. | Speeches, addresses, etc., American.
Classification: LCC E169.1.M1366 2017 | DDC 973—dc23 LC record available at https://lccn.loc.gov/2017002640

ISBN 978-1-5011-7421-6
ISBN 978-1-5011-7419-3 (pbk)
ISBN 978-1-5011-7420-9 (ebook)

For Our Grandchildren

Caitlin

Jed

Tyler

David

Leah

Ethan

Jesse

Caroline

William

Melissa

Geoffrey

Nellie

Louisa

Henry

Rosie

Nathaniel

Tamaelle

Luke

May

"Perseverance and spirit have done wonders in all ages."

—GEORGE WASHINGTON

Contents

Introduction

History, I like to think, is a larger way of looking at life. It is a source of strength, of inspiration. It is about who we are and what we stand for and is essential to our understanding of what our own role should be in our time. History, as can't be said too often, is human. It is about people, and they speak to us across the years.

Our history, our American story, is our definition as a people and a nation. It is a story like no other, our greatest natural resource, one might say, and it has been my purpose in my work to bring that story and its protagonists into clearer, more human focus in what I have written and in speeches I have made.

The speeches included here have been selected from a great

many given over the past twenty-five years with the hope that what I have had to say will help remind us, in this time of uncertainty and contention, of just who we are and what we stand for, of the high aspirations that inspired our founders, of our enduring values, and the importance of history as an aid to navigation in such troubled, uncertain times.

Two of the speeches were delivered at celebrations of national anniversaries—the Bicentennial of the United States Congress and the Bicentennial of the White House. Two others were given on historic ground and at ceremonies honoring two eminently memorable American experiences, one of high hopes, the other of tragic loss and words of everlasting value.

The first was a summer naturalization ceremony at Thomas Jefferson's Monticello. The second, a memorial service marking the fiftieth anniversary of the assassination of John F. Kennedy, took place at midday, November 22, 2013, at Dealey Plaza in Dallas, Texas. More than five thousand people had gathered, many having traveled far to be there. The day was miserable—cold, wet, and windy—and the crowd had been gathered since early morning. The Naval Academy Glee Club sang "The Battle Hymn of the Republic." The scene from the speaker's platform was one I will never forget.

University and college campuses have been the setting for a number of the other speeches included, and at those occasions I hoped to make clear to the young men and women about to step in to full participation in American life the vital importance of knowing their country's history, but also that history, like music, like poetry, like art, is a wonderful way to enlarge the experience of being alive—and that history is not about politics and war only, not by any means, and for the reason that music and poetry and art are very much a part of history, a point of particular emphasis in the talk I gave at Lafayette College in 2007.

I have no idea how many speeches I've given, starting at least fifty years ago, but I do know I have spoken in all fifty states and I am still at it, primarily because I feel I have something to say and because I always enjoy seeing our country and meeting people and listening to what they have to say.

Yes, we have much to be seriously concerned about, much that needs to be corrected, improved, or dispensed with. But the vitality and creative energy, the fundamental decency, the tolerance and insistence on truth, and the good-heartedness of the American people are there still plainly.

Many a time I have gone off on a speaking date feeling a bit down about the state of things and returned with my outlook greatly restored, having seen, again and again, long-standing American values still firmly in place, good people involved in joint efforts to accomplish changes for the better, the American spirit still at work.

Simon Willard's Clock

JOINT SESSION OF CONGRESS
Washington, D.C.
1989

Mr. Speaker, Mr. Vice President, Senator Dole, Members of the 101st Congress, ladies and gentlemen. For a private citizen to be asked to speak before Congress is a rare and very high honor and I thank you.

Simon Willard was never a Member of Congress in the usual sense. Simon Willard of Roxbury, Massachusetts, was a clockmaker early in the nineteenth century and he did it all by hand and by eye.

"In cutting his wheel teeth," reads an old account, "he did not mark out the spaces on the blank [brass] wheel and cut the teeth to measure, but he cut, rounded up and finished the teeth

IN GOD WE TRUST

David McCullough addressing Congress

as he went along, using his eye only in spacing, and always came out even. . . .

"It is doubtful," the old account continues, "if such a feat in mechanics was ever done before, and certainly never since."

The exact date is uncertain, but about 1837, when he was in his eighties, Simon Willard made a most important clock. I will come back to that.

On a June afternoon in 1775, before there was a Congress of the United States, a small boy stood with his mother on a distant knoll, watching the battle of Bunker Hill. The boy was John Quincy Adams, diplomat, senator, secretary of state, and president, who in his lifetime had seen more, contributed more to the history of his time than almost anyone and who, as no former president ever had, returned here to the Hill to take a seat in the House of Representatives, in the 22nd Congress, and thrilled at the prospect. And it was here that this extraordinary American had perhaps his finest hours.

Adams took his seat in the old House—in what is now Statuary Hall—in 1831. Small, fragile, fearing no one, he spoke his mind and his conscience. He championed mechanical "improvements" and scientific inquiry. To no one else in Congress are we so indebted for the establishment of the Smithsonian Institution. With Congressman Abraham Lincoln of Illinois and Thomas Corwin of Ohio, he cried out against the Mexican War, and for eight long years, almost alone, he battled the infamous Gag Rule imposed by southerners to prevent any discussion of petitions against slavery. Adams hated slavery, but was fighting, he said, more for the unlimited right of all citizens

The House of Representatives by Samuel F. B. Morse

to have their petitions heard, whatever their cause. It was a gallant fight and he won. The Gag Rule was permanently removed.

Earlier this year, at the time of the inaugural ceremonies of George Herbert Walker Bush, I heard a television commentator broadcasting from Statuary Hall complain of the resonance and echoes in the room. What resonance! What echoes!

John Quincy Adams is a reminder that giants come in all shapes and sizes and that, at times, they have walked these halls, their voices have been heard, their spirit felt here. Listen, please, to this from his diary, from March 29, 1841:

> *The world, the flesh, and all the devils in hell are arrayed against any man who now in this North American Union shall dare to join the standard of Almighty*

God to put down the African slave trade, and what can
I, upon the verge of my seventy-fourth birthday, with
a shaking hand, a darkening eye, a drowsy brain, and
with all my faculties dropping from me one by one, as
the teeth are dropping from my head—what can I do
for the cause of God and man. . . .

And how he loved the House of Representatives:

The forms and proceedings of the House [he writes],
this call of the State for petitions, the colossal emblem
of the Union over the Speaker's chair, this historic Muse
at the clock, the echoing pillars of the hall, the tripping
Mercuries who bear the resolutions and amendments
between the members and the chair, the calls of ayes
and noes, with the different intonations of the answers,
from different voices, the gobbling manner of the clerk
in reading over the names, the tone of the Speaker in an-
nouncing the vote, and the varied shades of pleasure and
pain in the countenances of the members on hearing it,
would form a fine subject for a descriptive poem.

Some nights he returned to his lodgings so exhausted he could barely crawl up the stairs. In the winter of 1848, at age eighty, after seventeen years in Congress, Adams collapsed at his desk. A brass plate in the floor of Statuary Hall marks the place.

He was carried to the speaker's office and there, two days

later, he died. At the end Henry Clay in tears was holding his hand. Congressman Lincoln helped with the funeral arrangements. Daniel Webster wrote the inscription for the casket.

Many splendid books have been written about Congress: Harry McPherson's *A Political Education*, Allen Drury's *A Senate Journal*, Alvin Josephy's *On the Hill* and *Kings of the Hill*, by Representative Richard Cheney and Lynne V. Cheney, *Rayburn*, a fine recent biography by D. B. Hardeman and Donald Bacon, and *The Great Triumvirate*, about Clay, Webster, and Calhoun, by Merrill Peterson. Now, in the bicentennial year, comes volume one of Senator Robert Byrd's monumental history of the Senate.

But a book that does justice to the story of Adams's years in the House, one of the vivid chapters in our political history, is still waiting to be written as are so many others.

Our knowledge, our appreciation, of the history of Congress and those who have made history here are curiously, regrettably deficient. The plain truth is historians and biographers have largely neglected the subject. Two hundred years after the creation of Congress, we have only begun to tell the story of Congress—which, of course, means the opportunity for those who write and who teach could not be greater.

There are no substantial, up-to-date biographies of Justin Morrill of Vermont, author of the Land Grant College Act; or Jimmy Byrnes, considered the most skillful politician of his day; or Joe Robinson, the most tenacious Democratic majority leader, whose sudden death in an apartment not far from here meant defeat for Franklin Roosevelt's court-packing scheme;

or Carl Hayden of Arizona, who served longer in the Senate than anybody, forty-one years.

We have John Garraty's life of Henry Cabot Lodge, Sr., but none of Henry Cabot Lodge, Jr. Search the library shelves for a good biography of Alben Barkley or Speaker Joe Martin and you won't find one. They don't exist. The only biography of Senator Arthur Vandenberg ends in 1945, when his career was just taking off.

The twentieth-century senator who has been written about most is Joe McCarthy. There are a dozen books about

Margaret Chase Smith

McCarthy. Yet there is no biography of the senator who had the backbone to stand up to him first—Margaret Chase Smith.

"I speak as a Republican," she said on that memorable day in the Senate. "I speak as a woman. I speak as a United States Senator. I speak as an American. I don't want to see the Republican Party ride to political victory on the four horsemen of calumny—fear, ignorance, bigotry and smear."

We have books on people like Theodore Bilbo and Huey Long, but no real biographies of George Aiken or Frank Church.

Richard Russell of Georgia, one of the most highly regarded, influential figures to serve in the Senate in this century, used to take home old bound copies of the *Congressional Record* to read in the evenings for pleasure. He loved the extended debates and orations of older times and would remark to his staff how strange it made him feel to realize that those who had once counted for so much and so affected the course of American life were entirely forgotten.

You wonder how many who pour in and out of the Russell Building each day, or the Cannon Building, have any notion who Richard Russell was? Or Joseph Gurney Cannon? There is no adequate biography of either man.

As Speaker of the House and head of the Rules Committee, Uncle Joe Cannon, of Danville, Illinois, once wielded power here of a kind unimaginable today. He was tough, shrewd, profane, picturesque, and a terrible stumbling block. It was the new twentieth century. The country wanted change, reform. Uncle Joe did not. "Everything is all right out west and around Danville," he would say. "The country don't need any legislation."

When a bill came up to add a new function to the U.S. Commission of Fish and Fisheries, making it the U.S. Commission of Fish and Fisheries and Birds, Cannon protested. He didn't like adding "and Birds" . . . "and Birds" was new and different and therefore unacceptable.

The insurrection that ended Cannon's iron rule, a revolt here in this chamber in 1910, was led by George Norris, of Red Willow County, Nebraska. There have been few better men in public life than George Norris and few more important turning points in our political history. Yet today it is hardly known.

How much more we need to know about the 1st Congress when everything was new and untried.

How much we could learn from a history of the Foreign Relations Committee.

Imagine the book that could be written about the Senate in the momentous years of the New Deal. Think of the changes brought about then. Think of who was in the Senate—Robert Wagner, Burton K. Wheeler, Hugo Black, Claude Pepper, Barkley, Huey Long, Tom Connally, Vandenberg, Robert A. Taft, George Norris, William Borah of Idaho, and J. Hamilton Lewis of Illinois, a politician of the old school who still wore wing collars and spats and a pink toupee to match his pink Vandyke whiskers.

It was "Ham" Lewis who advised a newly arrived freshman senator named Truman from Missouri, "Harry, don't start out with an inferiority complex. For the first six months you'll wonder how the hell you got here, and after that you'll wonder how the hell the rest of us got here."

For some unaccountable reason, there is not even a first-rate history of the Capitol, nothing comparable say, to William Seale's history of the White House. This magnificent building grew in stages, as America grew. It is really an assembly of different buildings, representative of different times, different aspirations, and the story should be told that way.

We are all so accustomed to seeing our history measured and defined by the presidency that we forget how much of the story of the country happened here.

Beside Congress, the presidency seems clear, orderly, easy to understand. The protagonists are relatively few in number and take their turns onstage one at a time.

Here individuals come and go, terms overlap. The stage is constantly crowded. The talk and the rumpus go on and on. And there is such a lot of humbug and so much that has been so overwhelmingly boring.

But let no one misunderstand, and least of all you who serve here, we have as much reason to take pride in Congress as in any institution in our system. As history abundantly shows, Congress, for all its faults, has not been the unbroken parade of clowns and thieves and posturing windbags so often portrayed. We make sport of Congress, belittle it, bewail its ineptitudes and inefficiency. We have from the beginning, and probably we always will. You do it yourselves, particularly at election time. But what should be spoken of more often, and more widely understood, are the great victories that have been won here, the decisions of courage and vision achieved, the men and women of high purpose and integrity, and yes, at times genius, who have served here.

It was Congress after all that provided the Homestead Act, ended slavery, ended child labor, built the railroads, built the Panama Canal, the Interstate Highway System. It was Congress that paid for Lewis and Clark and for our own travels to the Moon. It was Congress that changed the course of history with Lend-Lease and the Marshall Plan, that created Social Security, TVA, the G.I. Bill, the Voting Rights Act, and the incomparable Library of Congress.

It is not by chance that we Americans have built here on our Capitol Hill, side by side with the center of government, our greatest library, a free and open repository of books and without limit on viewpoint, in every language, from every part of the world.

In two hundred years, 11,220 men and women have served in the House and Senate, and while the proportions of black Americans, of women, of Hispanic and Asian Americans, and Native Americans have not, and do not now, reflect the country at large, it is nonetheless the place where all our voices are heard. Here, as they say—here as perhaps we cannot say too often—the people rule.

We need to know more about Congress. We need to know more about Congress because we need to know more about leadership. And about human nature.

We may also pick up some ideas.

Considering the way defense spending has been handled

in recent years, we might, for example, think of reinstating an investigating committee like the Truman Committee of World War II, which saved billions of dollars and thousands of lives.

If we are unwilling to vote the taxes to pay for the war on drugs, to save our country, why not sell bonds as we did in two world wars? It is hard to imagine anyone not wanting to buy a bond to win the war on drugs.

Above all we need to know more about Congress because we are Americans. We believe in governing ourselves.

"The boy should read history," the first John Adams wrote to his wife, Abigail, about the education of their son John Quincy. We must all read history, and write and publish and teach history better.

How can we know who we are and where we are headed if we don't know where we have come from? How can we call ourselves patriots if we know little of our country's past?

Who were those people in the old bound volumes of the *Congressional Record*? What moved them? What did they know that we do not?

Our past is not only prologue, it can be bracing. In Emerson's words, "The world is young, the former great men [and women] call to us affectionately."

I have decided that the digital watch is the perfect symbol of an imbalance in outlook in our day. It tells us only what time it is now, at this instant, as if that were all anyone would wish or need to know. Which brings me back to Simon Willard.

In the years when the House of Representatives met in Statuary Hall, all deliberations were watched over by the muse of history, Clio. She is there still over the north doorway. She is riding the winged *Car of History*, as it is called, keeping note in her book. The idea was that those who sat below would take inspiration from her. They would be reminded that they, too, were part of history, that their words and actions would face the judgment of history, and that they could count themselves part of an honorable heritage.

The Car of History by Carlo Franzoni; clock by Simon Willard

Clio and the *Car of History* are by the Italian sculptor Carlo Franzoni of Carrara. The clock in the foreground is by Simon Willard. It was, as I said, installed about 1837. Its inner workings, cut freehand by Simon Willard, ticked off the minutes and hours through debate over the Gag Rule, the annexation of Texas, the Mexican War, tariffs, postal service, the establishment of the Naval Academy, statehood for Arkansas, Michigan, Wisconsin, matters related to immigration, the Gold Rush, statehood for California, the fateful Kansas-Nebraska Act, and the final hours of John Quincy Adams.

It is also a clock with two hands and an old-fashioned face, the kind that shows what time it is now . . . what time it used to be . . . and what time it will become.

Civilization and the City

UNIVERSITY OF PITTSBURGH

Pittsburgh, Pennsylvania

1994

What a day this is for all of us—for you who are graduating and for so many who've been with you along the way, all the generous providers and encouragers, the inspirers, the prodders, the believers in you—parents, sisters, brothers, husbands, wives, grandparents, roommates, teammates, faculty, coaches, loan officers. And librarians. And all the worthy street-level dispensers of books and sneakers and haircuts and midnight coffee and pizza to go.

For me, to be part of the day, to receive this highest of tributes from your university is a surpassing honor. For there is no recognition so sweet as in your hometown. I couldn't be more pleased or grateful.

So here we are. The time is midafternoon in the month of May, in the year 1994, so near the close of this tumultuous twentieth century, and over the horizon, a new and unknown century the name of which will take some getting used to.

The place is Pittsburgh, where the Monongahela meets the Allegheny to form the mighty Ohio, longitude 80 degrees west, latitude 40 degrees 26 north, Pittsburgh, Pennsylvania, one of our nation's best, most interesting, most promising cities. And it is this particular juncture of time and place and the promise of the American city that I wish to talk about.

Few places there are where past and future so vividly join forces as they do here. In ways distinctly its own, Pittsburgh has been both grounded in yesterdays and ahead of its time. Once it was the gateway to the west when the west was the future. The first general hospital, the first radio station, the first educational television station when founded here were all well in advance of their time and events of national importance. And so, of course, was the rise of the steel empire, with the advent of the Bessemer process, the enterprise that more than any other put Pittsburgh on the map and started the nation to industrial supremacy. The city's great cleanup of air and water beginning in the late 1940s became an example for the world, long before environmental concerns became fashionable. And while the old steel city, the Pittsburgh of my childhood, has vanished—the smoke and grime, the throbbing red skies at night, gone as much as the world war that kept the mills roaring then—the wonderful old neighborhoods survive as they don't in other places, treasured old churches, temples, bridges, the great courthouse. Historic preservation has succeeded here in ways to make the rest of the country take notice and take heart.

Your own Cathedral of Learning towers over Oakland still as it has since it was built. It rose out of the 1930s, out of the depths of the Great Depression, let us not forget, a symbol of the affirmation to a city especially hard hit by hard times.

The university that once, in the 1890s heyday of the steel barons, enrolled all of ninety-five upperclassmen, today, in the 1990s, graduates five thousand men *and* women. And, as my parents' generation would have found unimaginable, the university has replaced the steel empire as the largest employer in the city, while its economic impact on the community overall is greater than even the statistics suggest.

Remove Pitt from Pittsburgh and the loss would be devastating. But city and university are each enlarged, each inspired by the other, and the importance of the responsibility each owes the other is paramount. They are joined in a vital past, as Robert Alberts has shown in his fine history of the University of Pittsburgh. And, make no mistake, their futures, too, are joined. Each must make good on what it owes the other, what it can do to serve the best interests of the other.

Cities are civilization. And all great cities are great composites—more than marketplace only, or production or financial center only, or where we wine and dine or feel the lift of soul from great music, drama, and art, but all of these. In our

The Cathedral of Learning, University of Pittsburgh

cities are our vital centers of learning, law, scientific inquiry, publishing, the seats of government, our meeting places, medical centers, centers of ideas. Our whole way of life in America depends on our cities, on the heartbeat of places like Pittsburgh.

We are an outdoor-loving people. We sing of spacious skies and purple mountains and go off pioneering by four-wheel drive. We turn nostalgic about small towns and build ever more suburbs. But the strength of America, the great concentration of wealth, culture, opportunity, the great mother lode of human resources is in the American city, and the American city is in deep trouble. As a consequence, our way of life is threatened and more seriously than we seem willing to face.

We cannot escape this. We cannot possibly ignore it or cling to some foolish hope that somehow it will just go away.

What can be done, we ask—about violent crime? About drug addiction? About the epidemic spread of AIDS and its consequent suffering and loss? What can we do about the thousands of homeless in our streets? The continuing degradation of the poorest among us? And of their children most of all? What can we try? What will work?

I have a suggestion and it is this: We must enlist the power and resources of our universities in a new way.

As through the years of the Cold War our leading universities, with millions of dollars in federal support, were actively involved in research and development for military purposes, let the leading universities centered in our cities become actively involved in helping to understand and solve the terrible problems of our cities.

If there is to be a "peace dividend," let a substantial part of it be put to work for this purpose, in the form of major grants to our big-city universities to examine the troubles that persist where they are, to be resourceful, innovative, and so share more of the responsibility for the city's future. But "peace dividend" or no, let strong support come from the corporations, businesses, financial institutions, and foundations that have such a high stake in the city.

A Marshall Plan for the cities has been talked of repeatedly and so far has come to nothing. This could be the positive, creative first step.

And why not let it begin here in Pittsburgh, this city of firsts, with the University of Pittsburgh leading the way?

The core of such a program, I suggest, should be history, for the specific and realistic reason that all problems have histories and the wisest route to a successful solution to nearly any problem begins with understanding its history. Indeed, almost any attempt to solve a problem without an understanding of its history is to court failure—as example our tragic plunge into Vietnam with hardly a notion of its past.

What is the history of homelessness in Allegheny County? How much do we know about that? What has been the community-wide experience down the years with alcohol and drug addiction? What can be learned about community response to epidemic disease from the terrifying experience of 1919 when influenza swept western Pennsylvania? Or from the annals of violent crime here one generation to another?

Let the university marshal its resources, its immense, multiple capacities for investigation and analysis, its concentrated brain power to help. Let the surrounding city be the university's lab, its terrain for fieldwork, its case study to a degree far beyond anything done to date. Let there be a broad range of projects at both the undergraduate and graduate school levels—in history especially, but in other disciplines as well: economics, public health, government, urban studies, social work, environmental engineering.

The history of Pittsburgh is already part of the curriculum at Pitt, in a course taught by Professor Ted Muller. But it's only one course and limited to just forty students, about a third the number who would like to take it. I propose not only enlargement of Professor Muller's program, but the creation of much more.

At Yale in the 1940s, a new American studies program was launched, a new American studies department established, and the idea quickly spread to other universities. A new department of Pittsburgh studies could be Pitt's contribution now. And, yes, there would be a major in Pittsburgh studies.

The new department could draw on so much that the university already has in talented faculty. It could bring into focus and be the means of coordination for a variety of programs already concerned in part with the subject of Pittsburgh.

"Too limited intellectually," some might protest. No more limited than the study of anything. It all depends on who is teaching, who is inspiring students to think anew. The horizons of this protean city are after all worldwide.

Others might question the "market value" of such an

education. Where might one go with a degree in Pittsburgh studies? It's hard to imagine anyone graduating from the University of Pittsburgh well grounded in how this city works and not finding a welcome in business, government, education, here especially but elsewhere, too.

And think of the value to the community of twenty to forty or more graduating every year with Pittsburgh their specialty. Think of the accumulative value of research, of the gathering expertise over a period of ten or twenty years. Imagine the outpouring of ideas generated when students discover the excitement of breaking new ground in a field and have the added motivation of knowing that what they are doing is important.

Think what needless, costly mistakes might be avoided here and elsewhere in urban America if the idea of such university involvement were to catch on. In St. Louis, a new high-speed transit system to the airport was routed through a historic black cemetery because its importance to the black community wasn't understood or even considered, with the result that the project has come to a halt and no one knows how much money wasted.

You have to know what people have been through to understand what people want and what they don't want. That's the nub of it. And what people have been through is what we call history.

In 1996, a new Pittsburgh regional history center will open downtown, a combination museum, library, research, and archival facility. It will be a major new attraction for the city, the finest center of the kind in the country, and it could be the perfect adjunct to a new Pittsburgh studies program at Pitt. The opportunities couldn't be better, the time is right, the plans for such a joining of forces could begin at once.

The University of Pittsburgh's extraordinary trail blazing in medicine is known to the world. The newly announced University of Pittsburgh Press project to produce the twentieth-century literary works of the Caribbean and Latin America in excellent English translations is one of the most exciting and ambitious international publishing ventures ever. Bold innovation is a University of Pittsburgh tradition. As the Cathedral of Learning, a university concept like no other, became a symbol of affirmation in the dark times of the 1930s, let it be so again now, when so much that we hold dear about American life is at stake. Let's do something about it.

In that spirit, I say to you of the Class of 1994, you who are going on to graduate school, in order to pursue careers in the professions, you who will enter directly in the workforce, you couldn't be more welcome. *You couldn't be more needed.*

Be generous. Give of yourself. Have the courage of your convictions. And whatever path you take, whatever your work, enjoy it—because, for one thing, if you're happy, you'll think better.

The Spirit of Jefferson

INDEPENDENCE DAY NATURALIZATION CEREMONY AT MONTICELLO

Charlottesville, Virginia

1994

This is a thrilling occasion—for all of us, whoever we are, however little or far we've journeyed to be here. And it is for me a great privilege to speak to you who are today becoming citizens of the United States.

You are sixty-two in number and come from twenty-four countries. You begin now your new lives as Americans on this most American day of celebration, July 4th, the nation's birthday, and here at this beloved place called Monticello, home of the incomparable American who wrote what is rightly called the nation's birth certificate.

Monticello

Here Thomas Jefferson lived, here he died, in this house in his bedroom on the first floor and also on this, of all days, July 4th, in the year 1826.

In Massachusetts, on that same day, John Adams, too, died. And for much of the country, the timing was far more than a strange coincidence. For Americans everywhere, it was taken as a "visible and palpable manifestation" of "Divine favor," and who could blame them for thinking so.

In Philadelphia, fifty years earlier, in 1776—now two hundred and eighteen years ago—young Thomas Jefferson was one of a committee of five, including Adams, chosen to prepare a Declaration of Independence. But to Jefferson alone fell the task of putting it into words.

He had thought Adams should do it. But Adams insisted, telling him, "You can write ten times better than I can."

Jefferson was thirty-three, tall, six foot two, slim, reserved, brilliant, and homesick for his wife and child and this green mountaintop. But there he sat in a Windsor chair in the front parlor of his two-room rented quarters on the second floor of a brick house at the corner of Seventh and Market Streets. There he sat through sweltering Philadelphia summer days, working at a portable writing box of his own design. He had no library at hand, no supply of books to draw upon, this most bookish of men, and he needed none because, as he later explained, he wanted only to say what everyone already knew.

The object was "not to find out new principles, or new arguments," he said ". . . but to place before mankind the common sense of the subject, in terms so plain and firm as to command their assent. . . . Neither aiming at originality of principle or sentiment, nor yet copied from any previous writing, it was intended to be an expression of the American mind, and to give that expression the proper tone and spirit called for by the occasion."

"An expression of the American mind," he said. . . . He read seven languages. He was a lawyer, surveyor, ardent meteorologist, botanist, agronomist, archaeologist, paleontologist, Indian ethnologist, classicist, brilliant architect. Music, he said, was the passion of his soul, mathematics, the passion of his mind.

He wanted, in what he wrote, to be plain and in spirit to rise to the occasion, he said. And what an occasion!

The Revolutionary War had begun at Lexington and Concord more than a year before. So it was not a declaration of war that was wanted. To Jefferson the Revolution was more than a struggle for independence, it was a struggle for democracy, and thus what he wrote was truly revolutionary.

Why do some men reach for the stars and so many others never even look up? Thomas Jefferson reached for the stars:

> *We hold these truths to be self-evident, that all men are created equal, that they are endowed by their Creator with certain unalienable Rights, that among these are Life, Liberty, and the pursuit of Happiness.—That to secure these rights, Governments are instituted among Men, deriving their just powers from the consent of the governed. . . .*

Never, *never anywhere,* had there been a government instituted on the consent of the governed.

Was Jefferson including women with the words "men" and "mankind"? Possibly he was. Nobody knows. Was he thinking of black Americans when he declared all men are created equal? Ideally, yes, I think. Practically, no. He was an eighteenth-century Virginia planter, it must be remembered, as the slave quarters along Mulberry Row, just over there, attest. He was an exceedingly gifted and very great man, but like the others of that exceptional handful of politicians we call the Founding Fathers, he could also be inconsistent, contradictory, *human.*

And more important than how *he* interpreted his ringing

words is their sustaining power to inspire, beyond the influences of time and place.

"All honor to Jefferson," wrote Abraham Lincoln on the eve of the Civil War, "[all honor] to the man who, in the concrete pressure of a struggle for national independence by a single people, had the coolness, forecast, and capacity to introduce into a merely revolutionary document, an abstract truth, applicable to all men and all times."

All honor to Jefferson in our own world now. We can never know enough about him. Indeed, we may judge our own performance in how seriously and with what effect we take his teachings to heart. When he wrote the Declaration of Independence he was speaking to the world then, but speaking to us also, across time. The ideas are transcendent, as is so much else that is bedrock to what we believe as a people, what we stand for, so many principles that have their origins here, with the mind and spirit of Thomas Jefferson. Sadly, too many today take for granted public schools, freedom of religion, freedom of speech, equality before the law, forgetting that these were ever novel and daring ideas.

Once on a summer evening in Washington, about a year ago, I stood on the Truman Balcony at the White House, that architectural supplement to the South Portico made by President Truman in the late 1940s, in keeping, as he explained to a critical press, with Jefferson's designs for the University of Virginia.

It was President Truman, you will remember, who by

EXECUTIVE ORDER

ESTABLISHING THE PRESIDENT'S COMMITTEE ON EQUALITY OF TREATMENT AND OPPORTUNITY IN THE ARMED SERVICES

WHEREAS it is essential that there be maintained in the armed services of the United States the highest standards of democracy, with equality of treatment and opportunity for all those who serve in our country's defense:

NOW, THEREFORE, by virtue of the authority vested in me as President of the United States, by the Constitution and the statutes of the United States, and as Commander in Chief of the armed services, it is hereby ordered as follows:

1. It is hereby declared to be the policy of the President that there shall be equality of treatment and opportunity for all persons in the armed services without regard to race, color, religion or national origin. This policy shall be put into effect as rapidly as possible, having due regard to the time required to effectuate any necessary changes without impairing efficiency or morale.

2. There shall be created in the National Military Establishment an advisory committee to be known as the President's Committee on Equality of Treatment and Opportunity in the Armed Services, which shall be composed of seven members to be designated by the President.

3. The Committee is authorized on behalf of the President to examine into the rules, procedures and practices of the armed services in order to determine in what respect such rules, procedures and practices may be altered or improved with a view to carrying out the policy of this order. The Committee shall confer and advise with the Secretary of Defense, the Secretary

Truman's executive order desegregating the armed forces

executive order ended segregation in the armed services. On that evening, beside me, stood the highest ranking officer in the military services, General Colin Powell. We were looking across the Mall, past the Washington Monument to the Jefferson Memorial, which was just catching the last light of day. It is his favorite of all the memorials in Washington, the general told me. Then, slowly and with feeling he recited the line— "I have sworn upon the altar of God eternal hostility against every form of tyranny over the mind of man."

The Declaration of Independence was not a creation of the gods, but of living men, and, let us never forget, extremely *brave* men. They were staking their lives on what they believed, pledging as Jefferson wrote in the final passage, "our lives, our fortunes, our sacred honor." By honor they meant reputation, their good name. Their word, once given, would not be broken. It was their code of integrity, their code of leadership.

The year before his death, Jefferson presented to his granddaughter and her husband, Ellen and Joseph Coolidge, Jr., of Boston, the portable writing box he had used to draft the Declaration of Independence and while it was of no "particular beauty," its "*imaginary value,*" he assured them, was bound to increase with years. And so it is with so much that is real from the past. There is no possible reckoning of the "imaginary value" of this great house, these lovely grounds, just as there is no possible reckoning of the creative energy of Jefferson's mind or the enduring vitality of his high purpose, his faith in the people of America.

By reaching for the stars, Jefferson gave us all the impulse.

He liked to talk about the energy of an idea. At times he seemed all ideas, all energy. "It is wonderful how much may be done, if we are always doing," he said. And as few men and women ever have, he was always doing for his country.

It is in that spirit that I welcome you, our new fellow Americans. The nation is the richer for you. I hope you will travel your new homeland from end to end, see as much of it as possible, read its history, enjoy its music, read aloud its poetry. I hope that in the spirit of Thomas Jefferson you will remain open to new ideas, prize tolerance and common sense and a love of the earth and its abundance.

Which Way Forward

UNION COLLEGE

Schenectady, New York

1994

Once, in 1779, even before there was a nation, nearly a thousand people of the community petitioned for a college here and this was something that had never happened before, the first popular demand for higher education in America. Think of that!

And listen, please, to this lovely item from the New York *Evening Post*, datelined Schenectady, February 24, 1795:

> *The gentlemen who were appointed by the inhabitants*
> *of the town of Schenectady to make application to the*
> *Regents of the University of the State of New York for*

collegiate powers in this town, have returned and assure us that the Regents have granted a charter for a college to be called Union. . . . The students of the Academy pleased with the information and sensible of the many and great advantages which will accrue for the western and northern parts of the state and to themselves in particular expressed their satisfaction on the occasion by illuminating the Academy Hall, which made a brilliant appearance, and greatly displayed the taste of the young gentlemen. The whole business was conducted with decency and good order.

Try to imagine the time and place. In 1795 the president of the United States was George Washington. Albany had yet to become the capital of New York. The Erie Canal was still thirty years in the future.

Historic ground: The design of this noble campus, by the French architect Joseph Jacques Ramée, dating from 1813, was not only the first architectural plan for a college campus anywhere in all of America, predating Jefferson's design for the University of Virginia by six years, it represented a whole new outlook. The arrangement of buildings we see about us was a major event in American life and ideas—not the closed monastic seclusion of the medieval quadrangle, but an open plan, in keeping with the open spirit of the times and with the pioneering vision of Union's legendary president, Eliphalet Nott. It was to be a place of learning open to the west, up the valley of the Mohawk, open to the wide world, open to those who wished to enter, open to ideas and innovation. We gather this commencement Sunday, let us remember, at the first interdenominational college in America. We gather where French was added to the curriculum when that simply wasn't done, where engineering was included with the liberal arts as it had never been before on any American campus. We gather where the brave, indomitable Eliphalet Nott, in baccalaureate addresses, spoke out against slavery nearly a full half century before the Civil War.

From this campus, from other graduation ceremonies not greatly different from today's, have come teachers, farmers, writers, bankers, geologists and astronomers, diplomats, attorneys, college presidents, merchants, politicians, physicians, and soldiers, many of whom counted significantly in American life, sometimes affecting the course of history or the reach

Union College

Eliphalet Nott

of knowledge. One, from the Class of 1856, Captain Charles Elliott Pease, carried the terms of surrender from Grant to Lee at Appomattox. Another from the same class, George Hough, discovered six hundred new double stars. There was William H. Seward, Class of 1820, who became Lincoln's secretary of state, and David Murray, from the Class of 1858, who became superintendent of educational affairs in the Japanese government. And if Chester A. Arthur, Class of 1848, is not one of our best-known presidents of the United States, he was unquestionably one of the tallest and best-tailored, a solid, well-meaning chief executive all-in-all, and the first ever to walk over the Brooklyn Bridge.

But what of the Class of 1994? What might be said of America, of the world you enter, on this 12th day of June, so near the start of a new century? Where do we stand?

The Cold War that began before many of your parents were born and that influenced American policy and American life more even than yet we know, is at last over. In 1953, at the beginning of the Cold War, in an astonishingly prophetic statement in his farewell address to the country, President Harry S. Truman said:

> As the free world grows stronger, more united, more attractive to people of both sides of the Iron Curtain—and as the Soviet hopes for easy expansion are blocked—then there will come a time of change in the Soviet world. Nobody can say for sure when that is going to be, or exactly how it will come about, whether by revolution, or trouble in the satellite states, or by a change inside the Kremlin.
>
> Whether the Communist rulers shift their policies of their own free will—or whether the change comes about in some other way—I have no doubt in the world that a change will occur.
>
> I have a deep and abiding faith in the destiny of free men. With patience and courage, we shall someday move on into a new era.

And so, some forty years later, that change has come and within the Soviet empire and with astonishing, unexpected suddenness. No one was quite ready for it, no one prepared, and now, as "the new era" opens, no one seems to know quite what to do.

In its approach to world problems, in its foreign policy, America seems oddly at sea. Without an enemy, some are saying, we have lost our sense of direction. The old certainties don't serve any longer.

Meantime, the country is beset by crime, drugs, poverty, racial tensions, AIDS, illiteracy, the list grows longer by the day, while the horrors of Bosnia and Rwanda, the tensions over Haiti and Korea fill the headlines. There can be no knowing what to do abroad, other voices insist, until we know what to do at home.

We find ourselves worrying and taking stock as a nation, in ways we've not before. Who are we? What do we want? Which way forward? And what of our values? Is it only by our possessions that we wish to be known? Does what we have matter more to us than what we do?

No, I don't think so. I think what most of us want—as most people everywhere want more than anything—is to be useful. This and to feel we belong to something larger than ourselves. What is needed now, now especially in this momentous change of scenes in world history, is a common understanding of what that larger something can be. What we Americans need above all is leadership to define the national ambition. And in this you of the Class of 1994 must play a part.

If we are beset by problems, we have always been beset by problems. There never was a golden time past of smooth sailing only. When Harry Truman spoke of the need for courage and patience in this new era, he was speaking from experience.

Once, in the last century, in the Cambria Iron Works at Johnstown, Pennsylvania, after working for months to build an unorthodox new machine for steel production, the engineer in charge, John Fritz, said at last, "All right boys, let's start it up and see why it doesn't work."

It is with that very American approach to problems that I think we will find our course. Beware the purists, the doctrinaires. It has been by the empirical method largely, by way of trial and error, that we have come so far. America itself is an experiment and we must bear that always in mind.

We are here because of the grit and faith of the generations who have gone before. As Winston Churchill reminded us in a darker time, "We didn't come this far because we are made of sugar candy."

But there is no inspiring leadership any longer, you hear it said. This is hardly so. Consider the looming example of President Nelson Mandela, one of the most extraordinary figures of the whole century there at the vortex of one of the most important events of the century.

For twenty-seven years he was in prison. How many could have withstood that? How many could have survived, unbroken in body and spirit? For sixteen of those years, for as long as you who are graduating have been in school since kindergarten, he was denied newspapers or any access to radio or television.

Then in 1990 he was released and there he stood, straight and tall, and entirely clear of mind and purpose. And four years later, on May the 10th of this year, 1994, the whole world watched as he took the oath of office in Pretoria, ending 342 years of white domination, a symbol of liberation and hope for twenty million people living in the equivalent of the ninth century BC. And yes, we saw greatness, too, in the conduct and character of the white man he replaced, President F. W. de Klerk.

In our foreign policy as in our own national life we need less fanfare, less stagecraft and circumventing. We need to talk sense, to speak the truth, to work harder and stay faithful to our fundamental beliefs. We are, each of us, responsible for our own actions, but we also know it has been bedrock in our American creed, that without cooperation, without all of us working together, pulling together, we can't make it. And we need you, you of the Class of 1994, all of you with all your gifts and energy, and your ideals. "Yes, I am an idealist," said Woodrow Wilson. "That's how I know I'm an American."

On a rainy April night in 1917, President Woodrow Wilson went to Capitol Hill to ask the Congress for a declaration of war. Against all tradition, America was to become embroiled in conflict and resolution far beyond its borders. The American part in World War I proved decisive. And there could be no turning back, as Wilson knew—America had responsibilities in the world. With a second and still more terrible world war,

American power and American responsibility grew greater by far. And again there could be no turning back. But power is not the point, responsibility is the point and at the heart of responsibility always are moral choices. In what we do, in what we say, what we stand for, we must feel, as did the founders of the nation, as did the founders of this college, that it is the example of America that matters.

So on you go with our heartfelt congratulations. You have good minds, now go out and use them. Make a difference. There's more opportunity than ever, more than you've any notion. I am of a generation raised on the idea that we as a people can do just about anything we set our minds to. I still believe that.

Let's do something about public education. Let's stop the mindless destruction of historic America. Let's clean up our rivers and skies, and while we're at it, let's clean up our language—private and public and on the airwaves. Let's stop the dumbing and degrading and cheap commercial exploitation of American life.

Be generous—with your money, of course. But more important, give of yourself. Take an interest in people. Get to know people. Get to know what they've been through before you pass judgment. That's essential.

Read history. By all means read history. We are all where we are, each of us, because others helped. As my friend Dr. Samuel Proctor, former pastor of the Abyssinian Baptist Church in New York, likes to say, "If you see a turtle sitting on a stump, you know it didn't get there on its own."

Read books. Try to understand the reason why things happen, why they are as they are. If you see only the surface phenomena, then the world becomes extremely confusing, ever more unsettling. But if the reasons are understood there's a kind of simplicity that emerges.

Sometime, somewhere along the line, memorize a poem. Sometime, somewhere along the line, go out in a field and paint a picture, for your own pleasure. Sometime, somewhere along the line, plant a tree, buy your father a good bottle of New York state wine, write your mother a letter.

And sometime, somewhere along the line, do something for your country.

The Animating Spirit

DICKINSON COLLEGE

Carlisle, Pennsylvania

1998

We are of many backgrounds. We've come from many places, some very far, to celebrate achievement, high achievement old and new—the founding of Dickinson College more than two centuries ago and the commencement of its newest graduates, the great Class of 1998.

Dickinson College, let it be remembered, is older than the Declaration of Independence, older than the Constitution, older than the country. In 1773, this part of Pennsylvania was the western frontier. Philadelphia, the largest city in the colonies, had a population of maybe thirty thousand at most.

The Revolutionary War had only just ended by the time

the college had a charter in 1783, and it was in Philadelphia that the first trustees gathered to take the oath of office.

The charter ceremony took place in the home of the president of the state of Pennsylvania, John Dickinson. He was made president of the board and it was for him, as you know, that the college was named. Slim as a needle, pale as a ghost, he was also, it happened, the largest donor.

James Wilson, prominent Philadelphia attorney and a signer of the Declaration of Independence, drew up the charter. Other trustees included clergymen, educators, politicians, mostly from here in Carlisle.

John Dickinson by Charles Willson Peale

Benjamin Rush by Charles Willson Peale

But the driving force of the project, the animating spirit, was one of the most exceptional Americans of that exceptional age, Benjamin Rush of Philadelphia. Physician, professor, patriot, inexhaustible reformer, he set things in motion and set an example that couldn't be more appropriate for this occasion or better medicine for the times we live in. Indeed, I hope I can leave you with the conviction that Benjamin Rush ranks among the outstanding Americans of all time.

Imagine a man who in one life served in the Continental Congress . . . signed the Declaration of Independence . . . served as a physician with Washington's army

. . . who gave Thomas Paine the title for his fateful tract *Common Sense*

. . . who became, through his own writing, the most famous American doctor of his time

. . . who established the first free dispensary in America and devoted much of his own practice to caring for the poor

. . . who helped found Pennsylvania's first society in opposition to slavery and in a passionate treatise denouncing slavery warned, "Remember that national crimes require national punishments"

. . . who championed better education for women, improved prison conditions, and opposed capital punishment

. . . who published the first chemistry textbook in America and wrote what may have been the first description ever in an American book of the game of golf.

The complete collected writings of Benjamin Rush fill forty-five volumes in the Pennsylvania Historical Society Library. His interests were all-encompassing—smoking chimneys and earthquakes, ballooning, old age, diet, clocks and microscopes, cooking, posture, mineral springs, good government, and sugar maple trees.

He was also a vociferous champion of abstinence from hard or spirituous liquors—but then no one's perfect.

In truth he was something of a gadfly intellectually. As a scientist he too often jumped to conclusions with little to go on. As a physician his heart often surpassed his head, though maybe in a physician that's not an altogether bad thing.

And Rush, to be sure, was a man of his time—or more to the point, a physician of his time—whose answer to most ailments was a severe bleeding, in addition to terrible emetics and purges, leading some latter-day scholars to surmise that the real heroes were his patients.

Nor did he, any more than others, understand the causes of malaria and yellow fever, two of the most dreaded scourges of the day.

But let us not look down on anyone from the past for not having the benefit of what we know, or allow ourselves to feel superior. In my experience, the more one learns of that founding generation of Americans—and I mean the real flesh-and-blood human beings, not the myths—the larger they become, the more one wonders what we've lost, or are in grave danger of losing.

If in some ways the doctor's professional perception was no better than the norm of the eighteenth century, in other ways he saw beyond his time as almost no one did.

Seeing insanity as an illness, not a curse, he demonstrated in his care of the insane that kindness and pleasant surroundings went much farther than punishment and moral lectures.

He was fascinated by dreams long in advance of Freud and has been called justifiably the father of American psychiatry.

Far ahead of his time, he insisted on better sanitation and hygiene among the troops of the Continental Army as a way to check the spread of disease.

He was fascinated by the influence of the environment on health. He knew that physical health and mental outlook were somehow joined and he would have concurred heartily with last week's report from three of our universities that stress has much to do with catching colds and that people with close ties to friends and family are the least likely to catch colds. *The New York Times* subhead to the story—

"More friends, fewer sniffles"—was exactly the kind of thing Rush might have said.

His own family was large and close—there were thirteen children—and friends mattered greatly to the doctor. He was constantly doing favors for friends and corresponding at length, busy as he was. Two of his closest friends were John Adams and Thomas Jefferson, and it was he, Benjamin Rush, who worked out a reconciliation between the two after years of enmity when they refused to speak to one another. Rush himself considered it one of his best services to the country.

That this bright, industrious son of a Pennsylvania farmer and model son of the Enlightenment was also a devout Christian is essential to our understanding of him.

"To spend and be spent for the good of mankind is what I chiefly aim at," he once said, and what he preached was what he practiced to his dying day.

The part he played in the 1793 yellow fever epidemic is legendary. While thousands of people, including some of the doctors, fled the city in terror, Rush remained working among the sick and dying, without letup, with little or no sleep, seeing as many as a hundred patients a day wherever they were, until he, too, took ill and collapsed.

His devotion to his patients in normal times was hardly less. I've been reading the diary of a Philadelphia woman named Elizabeth Drinker, a Quaker wife and mother whose large household included two free black children, boys aged seven and eleven, who to her alarm had taken severely ill.

"Dr. Rush called," she recorded April 8, 1794. "Dr. Rush

here in forenoon . . . [despite] roads being so very bad," reads her entry for April 9. Dr. Rush called again on April 12, April 14, April 15, 17, 22, and 27, and on into the first week of May. By my count he made fifteen house calls on those two boys by the time they were out of the woods. And Elizabeth Drinker records, too, that she had finished reading five volumes on religious matters lent to her by Dr. Rush.

Yet for all that Benjamin Rush did, said, wrote, accomplished in his crowded days, nothing surpassed his role as teacher and educator. Profoundly influenced in his own youth by some of the greatest educators of the age—Samuel Davies of Princeton, William Cullen of Edinburgh—Rush held education to be the highest of callings and took to it, of course, ardently, all out. "Prudence," he liked to say, "is a rascally virtue."

In the good society, Rush held, a physician must be a teacher. As a professor of medicine he trained perhaps three thousand doctors and unquestionably raised the standard of what passed then for medical training.

Further, he wanted everybody to be educated in the basic rules of good health and saw no reason why the benefits of exercise, sensible diet, good hygiene shouldn't be part of everyone's course of study.

What he wanted above all in education was more regard for the same phrase he'd given Tom Paine—common sense. At his own commencement day at Princeton, Rush had heard the president of Princeton, Samuel Davies, charge the graduating class to "bravely live in the service of your *own* generation." To Rush it was only common sense to prepare the young for the realities of their own time, their own lives. "We teach [our children] what was done 2,000 years ago and conceal from them what is doing every day," he wrote.

Too much fuss was made over Latin and Greek, he said. He wanted French, German, the modern languages emphasized, a radical notion then. He wanted more attention paid to writing and public speaking and disdained arbitrary divisions between science and the arts. "Some of our best physicians have been poets," he told his son James, who was to become a noted doctor in his own time.

Rush's life was not without shadow and heartache. He was ridiculed for his "lunatic system of medicine," called "remorseless" by one newspaper editor, and blamed for thousands of deaths during the yellow fever epidemic. One of his own sons was severely mentally ill. Rush's response was entirely in character. He sued the newspaper editor for libel and when he won the case, he gave the money to charity. To the afflicted son, who was confined to a mental hospital for the remainder of his life, Rush gave unstinting care and attention.

Rush remained active to the end. He died in 1813. On hearing the news, John Adams wrote to Jefferson, "I know of no character living or dead who has done more real good in America."

In all human relations, Rush taught, it was good nature that mattered most. "In this quality," he wrote, "I include candor, gentleness, and a disposition to speak with civility and to listen with attention to everybody." Words to the wise then, but perhaps in our own day more than ever.

"Knowledge," he said, "must be universal." How fitting that the students of this, the college he founded, now come from every part of the world, twenty-two different countries, and that you of the senior class have spent time studying abroad in some thirty-one different countries.

Rush, with his animating spirit, set a standard for Dickinson and for education overall, and it seems to me that the components of that spirit were threefold: goodwill (or good nature, as he said); inexhaustible curiosity (it was this that made him so everlastingly interested in everything and everyone); and commitment—commitment to principle, commitment to service, to his country, and to the fundamental faith that education ought never ever stand still, in the country and in one's own life. It is an animating spirit that transcends time and let it ever be so.

. . . I am greatly honored to be able now to count myself an alumnus of Dickinson College. I thank you for that and for inviting me to take part in this wonderful occasion.

Warmest congratulations to you of the Class of 1998 and to your families. You wouldn't be here today if you hadn't worked hard and done well. Be assured the world needs you.

It's said that you and your generation are apathetic, that you care only for money, that idealism is in decline among you.

I don't believe it.

I offer a parting thought from the good Dr. Rush: "The American war [with Britain] is over," he said in 1786, "but this is far from being the case with the American revolution. On the contrary, nothing but the first act of the great drama is closed."

Like much that he said, it is as true today as ever.

The Lessons of History

UNIVERSITY OF MASSACHUSETTS

Boston, Massachusetts

1998

President Bulger . . . Chancellor Penney . . . members of the Board of Trustees . . . fellow honorees . . . distinguished faculty . . . members of the Class of 1998 . . . ladies and gentlemen . . .

I've been thinking what two beautiful words they are . . . *university* . . . and *Massachusetts*.

University: from the Latin meaning universal. *University*: an idea, an ideal going back more than a thousand years.

And *Massachusetts*: a good American—*native* American— word, from the Algonquin tongue going back perhaps farther still and meaning "near the green mountain."

Say them together: the University of Massachusetts. What a potent combination. One might think it could hardly be improved on ... But then add Boston ... The University of Massachusetts Boston. Pure music!

It might never have happened. That's among the most important lessons of history ... and of life. There is so much around us that might never have happened were it not for a host of qualities called imagination, commitment, courage, creativity, and determination in the face of obstacles—that maybe most of all.

There were seemingly good reasons why this university should never have happened. There was already the university at Amherst. There were already many universities in Boston, and weren't they enough? But there were men and women who thought otherwise, who were inspired by the idea of not just a public city university, but one of first rank, with a first-rank faculty, and not just for any city, but for Boston.

They made it happen, a strong public university in Boston founded on the sound principle that in a vital community, as in one's own life, education ought never be at a standstill.

Chancellor Penney in her letter inviting me to take part in your commencement—one of the most gracious letters I have ever received—used the word *numinous*. I looked it up to be sure. It's a good word. It means of or pertaining to the spirit or spiritually elevated.

Rising above the ancient city of Florence is the magnificent Santa Maria del Fiore, the great cathedral that burst from the age of the Renaissance in the early fifteenth century, well before Columbus sailed. It wasn't Gothic. It wasn't Romanesque. It was something new and there it is still, rising 350 feet into the sky, beautiful as ever, *truly numinous*.

The architect of the cathedral dome was the incomparable Brunelleschi. But when praised for his genius in what he had done, he said—and it's this I hope you'll remember—he said, the credit did not belong to him but to Florence.

The credit for this university, the credit for this joyous occasion belongs to Boston, like so very much else that has enlarged and enriched American life—great works of literature, architecture, music, great strides in science, new ideas, noble causes.

It was here in Boston that the first school in America was established, here that the American Revolution began, here that the abolition movement took hold. Leonard Bernstein and Martin Luther King were educated here. How very many gifted and intrepid souls have embarked from these very shores, figuratively and literally.

Once, near dusk, in the bitter cold of winter, a father and his young son embarked in secret from the beach just down the bay, not three miles from here. They were two future presidents of the United States, John Adams and eleven-year-old John Quincy Adams. The year was 1778, in the midst of the Revolutionary War.

John Adams was bound three thousand miles over the sea in the dead of winter, to seek French support for the American cause. And there was every reason why he could have refused the mission, why it need not have happened. No one sailed the

John Adams by Gilbert Stuart

Atlantic in winter if it could be avoided. Enemy cruisers lay in wait. Adams was leaving family, home, livelihood, everything he loved, risking his life, risking capture and who knew what horrors at the hands of the enemy.

He felt ill-suited for diplomacy and had no training or experience. He spoke no French, the language of diplomacy. He had never in his life laid eyes on a king or queen or foreign minister of a great power or set foot in a city of more than thirty thousand people.

But go he did. With his overriding sense of duty, his ardor for his country, there was never really any doubt of his going.

If he was new to diplomacy, so was every American. If he was unable to speak French, he would learn.

Adams did well on the far side of the Atlantic. He secured vital loans, he played a key part in the Treaty of Paris that ended the war, and served as the first American ambassador to Britain. The boy John Quincy, as it turned out, would travel all the way to St. Petersburg and back, an epic, unheard of adventure of the time and the start of a life of diplomatic missions in the service of our country.

The lessons of history are manifold.

Nothing happens in isolation. Everything that happens has consequences.

We are all part of a larger stream of events, past, present, and future. We are all the beneficiaries of those who went before us—who built the cathedrals, who braved the unknown, who gave of their time and service, and who kept faith in the possibilities of the mind and the human spirit.

An astute observer of old wrote that history is philosophy taught with examples. Harry Truman liked to say that the only new thing in the world is the history you don't know.

From history we learn that sooner is not necessarily better than later . . . that what we don't know can often hurt us and badly . . . and that there is no such thing as a self-made man or woman.

A sense of history is an antidote to self-pity and self-importance, of which there is much too much in our time. To a large degree, history is a lesson in proportions.

History reminds us that nothing counterfeit has any staying power, an observation, incidentally, made by Cicero about 60 BC.

History teaches that character counts. Character above all.

I am extremely grateful for this high honor from the university and proud to count myself an alumnus now. To you the graduating class, warmest congratulations.

You're here because you've done a lot of hard work. Me too.

But more than most, I know, you've shown great determination to achieve what you have. And I have some idea of how many reasons there were that this day might never have happened in your life.

So on you go. If your experience is anything like mine, the most important books in your life you have still to read.

And read you will. Read for pleasure. Read to enlarge your lives. Read history, read biography, learn from the lives of others. Read Marcus Aurelius and Yeats. Read Cervantes and soon; don't wait until you're past fifty as I did. Read Emerson and Willa Cather, Flannery O'Connor and Langston Hughes.

Read a wise and sparkling book called *While the Music Lasts* by an author named William Bulger. See especially page 19, where he describes his own discovery of books.

The world needs you. There is large work to be done, good work, and you can make a difference. Whatever your life work, take it seriously and enjoy it. Let's never be the kind of people who do things lukewarmly. If you're going to ring the bell, give the rope one hell of a pull.

I wish you the fullest lives possible—full of love and bells ringing.

What's Essential Is Invisible

DARTMOUTH COLLEGE
Hanover, New Hampshire
1999

We have had farmers and generals in our highest office, and a great many lawyers, a college president, a world-famous engineer, numerous career politicians, and a movie star: and the movie star was by no means the only actor. Or necessarily the best one. Six of our presidents—and they were all men, all white men to be more specific—came from Ohio. There have been a number of Episcopalians, still more Presbyterians, and one Roman Catholic. Abraham Lincoln was the tallest at six foot four. James Madison was the smallest, at five foot four, and he weighed only a hundred pounds.

In striking contrast, William Howard Taft, by far the largest of the lot, weighed 332 pounds. A custom-built bathtub had to be installed in the White House. There's a wonderful old photograph in which the three workmen who did the installation sit together quite comfortably in Taft's giant tub. With Taft we had a gravitas of a kind, if not necessarily power, in the highest office.

Calvin Coolidge is famous for having said as little as possible. Theodore Roosevelt could hardly keep quiet.

Theodore Roosevelt was the youngest president in history. When he took office, after the death of McKinley in 1901, he was all of forty-two.

TR was the first president born in a big city. Harry Truman was the first and only president born in Missouri and the only president in this century who never went to college. It was not until Jimmy Carter that we had a president who was born in a hospital. John Adams, first of the Harvard men, was ninety at the time of his death in 1826.

Of the first seven presidents, whose combined terms spanned forty-eight years, all were slave masters but two, and they were father and son, John and John Quincy Adams. So for nearly half a century, slave holders dominated in the executive branch.

Presidential nicknames through the nineteenth century favored an affectionate use of the word "old" as a prefix—as in Old Man Eloquent (for John Quincy Adams), Old Hickory (for Andrew Jackson), Old Rough and Ready (for Zachary Taylor). In the twentieth century, beginning with TR, the use of initials became the fashion.

A great variety of wise and stirring pronouncements were delivered by, or attributed to our presidents, but then nearly all said some silly things, too. Jefferson stood on a hillside at Harpers Ferry where the Shenandoah meets the Potomac and proclaimed the view worth a trip to Europe. Gerald Ford, one of the most admirable presidents of our time, once observed that if Lincoln were alive today, he'd be turning over in his grave.

With few exceptions, they've all done a good deal of complaining about the job and professed no liking for it. It was so from the very beginning. George Washington went to his place at the head of the new government, "accompanied," he said, "by feelings not unlike those of a culprit who is going to the place of his execution." John Adams, Washington's successor, describing his inauguration to his wife, Abigail, wrote, "A solemn scene it was indeed and it was made more affecting to me by the presence of the General [Washington], whose countenance was as serene and unclouded as the day. Me thought I heard him say, 'Aye, I am fairly out and you are fairly in. See which of us is the happiest.'"

Jefferson famously declared the presidency a "splendid misery." Andrew Jackson called it "dignified slavery." Polk said it was "no bed of roses." Abraham Lincoln thought himself unfit for the role. Grover Cleveland told a very young FDR when they met, "Boy, I hope you will never, ever become president." Harry Truman privately referred to the White House as "the great white jail."

The first ladies of the land often took an equally dim view

of the part they had to play and worried incessantly over the stress their husbands were under. Perhaps the most memorable of recorded declamations on the subject of the presidency was made by Bess Truman during her one and only press conference. I will read it to you verbatim. The questions, I should explain, were written in advance and she answered them before the "ladies of the press" who were invited to the White House.

> "What qualities did she think would be the greatest asset to the wife of a president?"
> "Good health and a well-developed sense of humor."
> "Do you think there should ever be a woman President of the United States?"
> "No."
> "Would you want to be President of the United States?"
> "No."
> "Would you want Margaret ever to be First Lady?"
> "No."
> "If she had a son, would you try to bring him up to be President?"
> "No."
> "If it had been left to your own free choice, would you have gone into the White House in the first place?"
> "Most definitely not."
> "What was her reaction to the musical criticism of Margaret singing?"
> "No comment."

"Did any of the demands of her role as first lady ever give her stage fright?"

"No comment."

"What would you like to do and have your husband do when he is no longer President?"

"Return to Independence."

But the professed wish to go home again is also part of the tradition, going back to George Washington's longing for Mount Vernon. They've nearly all longed to return to whence they came, or so they said. But then rare was the man who truly wished to let go of the office. Most would have fought to their last breath to stay if they could.

Only TR openly declared his love for the job. "Nobody ever enjoyed the presidency as I did," he boasted, and by all evidence that was so. "While president I have been president emphatically," he said.

It's become commonplace to stress how the office has expanded. Yet the change is indeed startling.

When Jefferson was president he had a staff of somewhere between four and twelve people—in total. His salary, as it had been for Washington and Adams, was $25,000. Let me give you a few present-day statistics about the office. It pays $200,000 a year—taxable—but includes an annual expense allowance of $50,000, which is nontaxable. Then there's an additional expense account of $12,000 for official entertaining.

The total payroll for the executive branch, which includes all cabinet-level positions and those departments, 2,750,000 people, comes to nine and a quarter billion dollars. The White House staff, that is, the immediate staff of the president—what in Jefferson's day was a half dozen or so—is now 382 at a cost of $1,640,000.

The perks include a helicopter, Air Force One, and a fleet of thirty-five limousines. There is a White House swimming pool, tennis court, gymnasium, bowling alley, and in the Clinton years, a jogging track. The president also has two movie theaters, recording facilities, a library. There are riding horses supplied by the army, should he wish them, a private, armor-plated Pullman car, and some two thousand Secret Service agents on call for his protection.

He and his family live rent free, it should also be noted. Annual maintenance and operation of the house runs to eight million dollars and requires still another staff of more than a hundred maids, cooks, butlers, gardeners, and electricians. There is a Director of Systems Management for electronic mail, a Director of the Gift Unit, a Deputy Director of White House Gifts, a Manager of Data Entry Night Force, among others.

Then there's Camp David, which several presidents have hardly used at all. Harry Truman, for instance, thought it boring and wanted never to go there. The cost of Camp David runs to about a million dollars a year.

One of the best indices of what's happened to the scale of operations in recent years are the presidential trips to China, which have become obligatory. According to *The New York Times*, when President Nixon first went to China in 1972, his retinue numbered 300. Three years later, when President Ford made the trip, 450 went along. By 1984, when Ronald Reagan went, he took 600. Then came a temporary dip in the curve in 1989 when the number accompanying George Bush dropped back to 500. But in 1998 when Clinton made his trip, more than 1,000 went with him.

As John Steinbeck once wrote, "We give the President more work than a man can do, more responsibility than a man should take, more pressure than a man can bear." But we also give him more power, far more power, than has been held by any mortal in all history and a commensurate lot of swash, the show of power, to go with it. No king of England, no oriental potentate of old ever arrived with a greater display of his importance than does the modern president of the United States—which is a long way from Thomas Jefferson walking to the Capitol for his inauguration.

The twentieth-century presidency begins with Theodore Roosevelt. He was like nobody who had ever been president before, and appeared on the scene just as the century was getting under way. Significantly, it was also just at the point when it became technically possible to reproduce photographs in newspapers and magazines. So immediately TR became the most photographed president in history until then—and usually in action, this made possible by improved camera technology. He was photographed with his family, photographed jumping his

Theodore Roosevelt at the Panama Canal

horse, hiking, playing tennis. James J. Hill, the railroad tycoon, who didn't care for Roosevelt, said all he ever did was pose for pictures and draw his pay.

Modern times caught up with the presidency then. TR was the first president to go down in a submarine, the first to go up in an airplane, the first to call it the White House, officially. Most importantly, he saw himself a *world* leader. America had no choice but to play a big part in the world, he preached.

He embraced the power of the presidency without hesitation, with open delight, and used it effectively and imaginatively. He said he liked power for what he could do with it.

Eager to display American sea power, he decided to send the fleet on a goodwill tour around the world. Told that Congress would refuse to appropriate the money, he said he had sufficient funds at hand to send the ships halfway; then it would be up to Congress to decide whether to bring them home again.

To many TR is the president who built the Panama Canal. He himself thought it was what he would be best remembered for. The canal was the biggest-ever American effort beyond our borders, a project of worldwide importance. In fact, it was one of the greatest American achievements in history, for which that whole generation rightfully took tremendous pride. No other country had either the will or the wherewithal to do such a mighty thing, it was said, or a man like the one in the White House to see that it was done right.

When TR went to Panama to inspect the work firsthand in 1906, it marked the first time a president had ever left the country while in office. As might be expected, he went by battleship. The days he toured the "diggings" were among the happiest of his life and can be seen now as a kind of set piece—a president perfectly cast for his time. The spectacle, like nothing ever seen anywhere on earth before, was of American know-how, American machinery, American money and political power accomplishing what nature had neglected to provide, "the dream of Columbus," a passage to India.

Roosevelt was photographed his every waking hour on the scene. It was the first great presidential photo opportunity in history. The picture has become a metaphor for the age. As possibly only he could, TR took the controls of a giant ninety-five-ton Bucyrus-Erie steam shovel, the most powerful thing of its kind ever built, while wearing a spotless white linen suit. And so there he is, the commander-in-chief at the helm of "the biggest work that's ever been done," as he told the Americans on the job.

But it should be remembered, too, that he'd "taken" the Isthmus, as he said, with a high-handed use of power against the nation of Colombia. As he said in a speech, "I took the Isthmus, started the canal and then left Congress not to debate the canal, but to debate me." There's a raw kind of arrogance to that. There's also a raw truth to it. And the country, as it happened, loved it.

He was the most popular president we had had until then, and few since have had quite the same kind of hold on the popular imagination. He gave the country a good time just being himself. But importantly he *used* his popularity. He didn't just want it for the sake of being popular. He wanted it to do things. It was power he could make use of.

At the time of the great Anthracite Coal Strike of 1902, he stepped in as no president had, brought the executive branch of the government into labor arbitration for the first time, settled the strike, and transformed labor relations thereafter.

But then he entered into nearly everything. He was ebullient, confident, full of ideas, interested in everything, seldom without a book. He read books, he wrote books. He wrote his own messages to Congress. He wrote his own speeches.

In nearly eight years in office he initiated the first successful antitrust suit against a corporate monopoly. He doubled the size of the navy, helped settle the Russo-Japanese War, established five national parks, including the Grand Canyon, and made conservation a popular cause for the first time.

It's often remarked that the great presidents have been those who served in times of great crisis. And that might be taken as the rule were it not for the stunning exception of Theodore Roosevelt, who was president when there was no crisis, when, in fact, he could easily have coasted in the job, as some had done before him. But he was Theodore Roosevelt and that's the point.

At the heart of history, and a great part of the pull of history, is the mystery of human nature. And human nature—individual personality, makeup, call it what you will—has to be reckoned as a prime force in any consideration of the presidency and its power.

You may remember the scene in Saint-Exupéry's *The Little*

Prince when the fox says that what's essential is invisible. And so it is with this large subject of presidential power: To a very large extent it's invisible.

It has to do with aspects of individual personality for which there are no ready measurements—the integrity of Washington, Lincoln's depth of soul, the courage of Harry Truman. Or think of the charm of Kennedy at a press conference, or Ronald Reagan in front of a television camera in almost any circumstance.

Maybe if we could put presidential power in a pot and boil it all down, a big part of what we would find at the bottom would be language, the use of language, the potency of words. Power to persuade is power indeed and only a relative few of the pres-

Ronald Reagan

Franklin D. Roosevelt

idents had it—Lincoln, TR, Woodrow Wilson, and Franklin
Roosevelt. And JFK. His inaugural address didn't just thrill
the country then, it still does. The language transcends time.

Sometimes just a line—a single line—spoken by a president can do wonders. Think, for example, when at his inaugural Jimmy Carter said, "For myself and for our nation, I
want to thank my predecessor for all he has done to heal our
land." What a moment it was for the country. It got the new
Carter administration off to exactly the right start. The glow
of good feeling wouldn't last very long, but there it was and it
was just right.

One of my favorite lines from an inaugural address is this—I wonder if you remember who said it? "How can we love our country and not love our countrymen? And loving them, reach out a hand when they fall, heal them when they're sick, and provide opportunities to make them self-sufficient so they will be equal in fact and not just in theory." It was said by Ronald Reagan.

And a further point about Kennedy that strikes me as refreshing: He almost never talked about himself. The first-person singular almost never entered into anything he said, in contrast to so many others since. It was a big part of his appeal, I think.

Theodore Roosevelt not only called the presidency the "bully pulpit," he saw and demonstrated that the pulpit is the essence of the power of the office.

Harry Truman was saying much the same thing when, in a fit of exasperation, he tried to dismiss the whole notion of presidential power:

> *Aside from the impossible administrative burden, he, the President, has to take all sorts of abuse from liars and demagogues. The people can never understand why the president does not use his supposedly great power to make them behave. Well, all the President is, is a glorified public relations man who spends his time flattering, kissing and kicking people to get them do what they are supposed to do anyway.*

Truman was neither brilliant nor eloquent. He did not have the gift to move the country with words, to lift us up to do something bigger, nobler, to rise to a "rendezvous with destiny," the way his predecessor, Franklin Roosevelt, could. Roosevelt was extraordinary in that way through the worst depression in history and the most terrible of wars.

It was then, almost overnight as history goes, that the size, scope, the expenditures of government grew by geometric proportions, and with it the importance—or power—of the presidency. What is so difficult for many today to understand is that in the 1930s the United States was neither rich nor a military power. The army stood twenty-sixth in the world in strength, behind Switzerland and Argentina. And a good 40 percent of all the families in America were living on incomes of less than a thousand dollars a year. This, mind you, wasn't two hundred years ago, but within the memory of many of us here in this room. The whole idea of a rich, all-powerful nation-state with a standing army surpassing that of any on earth is something relatively new to American life.

With Truman's presidency in 1945 came the advent of nuclear weapons and the Cold War, the creation of the CIA, the National Security Council, a burgeoning Defense Department, NATO, and a fearsome, stepped-up arms race with the Soviets.

As Truman saw the presidency, the chief responsibility was to make decisions and he made some of the most difficult and far-reaching of any president. If not brilliant or eloquent, he was courageous and principled. The invisible something he brought to the office was character.

Harry and Bess Truman

He also demonstrated, and dramatically at times, what power—he would have said "authority"—rests with the president constitutionally, what a president can do by merely signing his name.

His most sensational and controversial decision was to fire General MacArthur, which was done on the perfectly sound premise, as set forth in the Constitution, that no one but the president is commander-in-chief of the armed forces. His subordinate, MacArthur, was disobeying orders, flagrantly—and indeed, if you go over the record, you wonder that Truman didn't fire him sooner than he did. Outrage in the country was stupendous. MacArthur was an authentic American hero, the greatest American of his day, many passionately believed, and who was little Harry Truman to bring him down. The answer, of course, was that Harry Truman was president and in time the country would come to see that he had done the right thing, even in the face of seeing his popularity plummet.

Another notable example of courageous executive authority, and among Truman's most admirable decisions—and again at great risk of his popularity—was the executive order that made segregation in the armed forces illegal. The year was 1948, you'll remember, an election year. Friends and advisors warned that if he persisted in his civil rights program he was certain to lose in November. That being so, Truman responded, then he would be losing for a good cause. Again, as commander-in-chief, he had no need to go to Congress, he had only to take up his pen and he did.

Another, more recent, brave, and controversial exercise of presidential power was Gerald Ford's decision to pardon Richard Nixon, which, to my mind, was also the right thing to have done—not for Ford's political fortunes but for the country.

It should be said, too, it seems to me, that the power of the presidency and the long-range wisdom of several of our presidents may be found also in what they chose *not* to do. We don't give enough credit to presidents for what they don't do.

John Adams did not go to war with France at a time when a great part of the country was breathing fire for war. Politically it would have been Adams's easy path and greatly to his advantage. But he knew a war was the last thing the struggling new country needed and so refused to go along and there was no war.

Truman didn't use the atomic bomb in Korea in the face of tremendous pressure to do so. Eisenhower didn't go into Vietnam. These were vastly important decisions.

Sometimes I wonder if we make too much of our presidents. Might it be better if we ignored them a little more than we do? But then on the other hand, I don't think we can ever know enough about them, and particularly before putting them in the job. The truth is, of course, it makes an enormous difference who's in the White House.

The First to Reside Here

Mr. President, distinguished guests, ladies and gentlemen. The first president to move into what was then known as the President's House, John Adams, of Quincy, Massachusetts, arrived here at this entrance at midday, Saturday, November 1, 1800, at just about this time. Very little looked as we now see it. The new federal city of Washington was no city at all. The Capitol was only half finished. Except for a few nondescript stores and hotels in the vicinity of the Capitol, the rest was mostly tree stumps and swamp.

The house itself was still quite unfinished. Fires had to be kept burning in all the fireplaces to help dry the wet plaster. Only a few rooms were ready. Only one twisting back stairway connected the floors. Though the president's furniture had arrived, shipped from Philadelphia, it looked lost in these enormous rooms. The only picture hanging was Gilbert Stuart's full-length portrait of George Washington, which still hangs in the East Room.

These beautiful grounds did not exist. It was a different setting; it was a different country; and it was a different time. And in that age, no one ever knew when anyone was going to arrive anywhere for certain, including the President of the United States. So on that historic morning, two district commissioners were inside inspecting the work when they happened to look out the window and commented, "There is the President of the United States." He had just rolled up in his carriage.

With him was his secretary, Billy Shaw, and one servant on horseback, John Brisling, who became the first steward of the White House. There was nobody else. No honor guard, no band playing, no entourage of any kind. But who was that man that walked through these doors, the first of forty presidents who have lived here thus far?

Adams had just celebrated his sixty-first birthday two days before, en route from Philadelphia. He was about five foot seven, about middle size in that day, and stout, but physically very strong. He stood erect, shoulders back. He was accustomed to building stone walls and bringing in the hay. He was a farmer's son, descended from four generations of plain, God-fearing New England farmers, and proud of it.

On missions to Europe in the midst of war, Adams traveled farther and under more adverse conditions in the service of his country than any American of the time, by far. It was John Adams who secured the desperately needed loans from the Dutch to help finance the war. He was a signer of the Paris peace treaty that ended the war, and the first American to appear before King George III, as a minister for the new United States of America.

Between times he also drafted the oldest written constitution still in use in the world today—the constitution of the Commonwealth of Massachusetts, written ten years before our own Constitution, and had great influence on the national Constitution. He was our first vice president, under George Washington, and elected president in 1796, defeating his old friend Thomas Jefferson.

John Adams could be proud, vain, irritable, short-tempered. He was also brilliant, warmhearted, humorous, a devoted husband and father, and a lifelong talker—an all-out, full-time talker. He loved *Don Quixote*. He loved the English poets. He carried a book with him everywhere he traveled.

He never had any money to speak of, and he is the only presidential Founding Father who, as a matter of principle, never owned a slave. Further, John Adams had the immense good fortune to be married to Abigail Smith Adams, one of the most extraordinary Americans of that extraordinary era. And their letters to one another constitute a national treasure.

John Adams was a great man and a highly principled president in tumultuous times. Though gravely mistaken when he signed the infamous Alien and Sedition Acts, he had the good sense and determination and courage to keep America from going to war with France, which was a very great accomplishment, indeed, with far-reaching consequences.

But let us not forget, too, that it was John Adams who nominated George Washington to be commander-in-chief of the Continental Army. It was John Adams who insisted that Jefferson be the one to write the Declaration of Independence. And it was President John Adams who made John Marshall chief justice of the Supreme Court. As a casting director alone, he was brilliant.

Abigail Adams did not arrive here to join her husband until two weeks later, in that long-ago November. She could never get over the size of the house. She called it the castle, and hung her laundry out to dry in the then unfinished East Room. The Adamses lived in the house less than four months, and it was not a happy time for them. Adams learned of his defeat for reelection by Jefferson in what was perhaps the most vicious presidential campaign in our history. Then, within days he and Abigail received the word—devastating word—that their second son, Charles, had died in New York of alcoholism.

There were men and women in that day, in their time, who would have refused to have lived in the White House in the condition it was in. But the Adamses made do without complaint. On January 1, 1801, they held the first New Year's Day reception here ever—an open house.

On his first evening in this house, following a light supper, John Adams retired early for the night. We may picture him with a single candle climbing that twisting back stairway. Early the next morning he went to his desk on the second floor and addressed a now famous letter to Abigail. Franklin Roosevelt thought so highly of the letter, and of two sentences in it, that he had it carved into the wooden mantelpiece in the State Dining Room. And when Harry Truman supervised the rebuilding of the White House, he insisted that that inscription remain where it is today.

When John F. Kennedy was president, he had the inscription carved into the mantelpiece in marble. "I pray heaven," Adams wrote, "to bestow the best of blessings on this house, and all that shall hereafter inhabit it. May none but honest and wise men ever rule under this roof."

John Adams's inscription on the White House mantelpiece

John Adams lived another twenty-five years, to age ninety.

A few days before his death, a delegation of his Quincy neighbors came to call on him. The old president sat in an armchair in his library as they asked if he could give them a toast that they might read aloud at the town's 4th of July celebration. "I will give you," said Adams, "independence forever." Asked if he would like to add something more to that, he said, "Not a word."

That was the man who first occupied the White House. I think how pleased he and Abigail would be if they were here to see how we've gathered today. To see the country they so loved still independent, still united and thriving, still strong, still free, and this grand old house looking so magnificent. But then, maybe they *are* here with us today.

History Lost and Found

NATIONAL TRUST FOR HISTORIC
PRESERVATION CONFERENCE

Providence, Rhode Island

2001

Carpenters' Hall sits out of the way of the flow of traffic between Third and Chestnut Streets in Philadelphia, back maybe two hundred feet in what's called Carpenters' Court. To me it's one of the most eloquent buildings in all of America.

It's very close to Independence Hall and Independence National Historical Park in Philadelphia. But many people walk right by and don't see it, which is a shame. It was finished before construction began of this church [the First Baptist Church, Providence, Rhode Island]. They are contemporaries and express the same sense of balance and light,

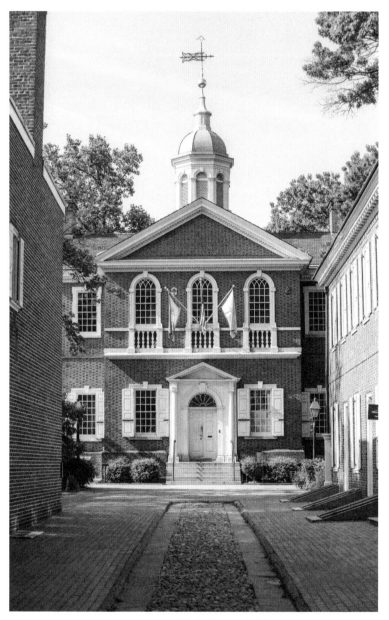

Carpenters' Hall, Philadelphia

balance and light being two of the great themes of the Enlightenment.

Carpenters' Hall was built by the Philadelphia Carpenters' Company, which was dedicated to fine workmanship and integrity in building. The Philadelphia Carpenters' Company still owns Carpenters' Hall. It was the place where, upstairs, Benjamin Franklin established his Library Company, which evolved into the first public library in America. And certainly along with freedom of religion, access to books, to learning, free to the people, is one of the greatest of our institutions.

Carpenters' Hall, much more importantly, was the gathering place for the First Continental Congress in the summer of 1774. It is a place of a great, immeasurably important beginning and what is so eloquent about it is that it is so very small. It's only fifty by fifty feet square. You could put it inside this meetinghouse where we are today with room to spare.

And when you stand there, in that very real, authentic place, you feel the presence of that other time, that history in a way that would be impossible did it not exist.

John Adams was one of the fifty-six delegates who gathered in Carpenters' Hall in 1774, and as he wrote to his wife, Abigail, back in Massachusetts, he thought he had come to one of the greatest conclaves of the greatest minds of all time. He was amazed by the range and variety of talents on display. "The art and address of ambassadors from a dozen belligerent powers of Europe, nay, of a conclave of cardinals at the election of a Pope . . . would not exceed the specimens we have seen." Here were eloquence and acuteness equal to any. "Every question is discussed with moderation, and an acuteness and a minuteness equal to that of Queen Elizabeth's Privy Council," he wrote. (Hyperbole was a great part of the fun of living in the eighteenth century.)

But after being subjected to a month of such "acuteness and minuteness" over each and every issue at hand, irrespective of importance, Adams was weary to death, as he said. The business of Congress had become tedious beyond expression. "This assembly is like no other that ever existed. Every man in it is a great man—an orator, a critic, a statesman, and therefore every man upon every question must show his oratory, his criticism, and his political abilities.

"The consequence of this is that business is drawn and spun out to immeasurable length. I believe if it was moved and seconded that we should come to a resolution that three and two make five, we should be entertained with logic and rhetoric, law, history, politics, and mathematics concerning the subject for two whole days, and then we would pass the resolution unanimously in the affirmative."

To hold such a letter in your hands at about the same distance from your eyes as it would have been from Abigail Adams's eyes, or to read what she wrote to him holding her letters in hand, is to make a physical, tactile contact with those distant human beings. There's nothing quite like it. You feel their mortality. You feel a common bond with them as fellow human beings.

The Adams letters are nearly all in the Massachusetts Historical Society. They're written on rag paper and so they will last forever, if properly taken care of. And the importance of that experience to students, to scholars, to all of us, any of us, is irreplaceable—just as is the tactile connection we make in a space like Carpenters' Hall or this church.

These buildings, those people, it might be said, aren't aspects of the past at all. One might indeed surmise there's no such thing as the past. Adams, Jefferson, George Washington, they didn't walk about saying, "Isn't this fascinating, living in the past? Aren't we picturesque?" It was the present, their present. Not our present, their present. And we have to understand that.

Nor were they just like we are. Their present was part of a different time, and because of that, they were different from us. We have to take into consideration, for example, all they had to contend with that we don't even have to think about— all the inconveniences, discomforts, and fears. And the hard, hard work.

There are more than one thousand letters just between Abigail and John Adams. Abigail herself has left over two thousand letters. Think of that. And when you consider all she had to do just to get through a day—up at 5:00 in the morning, waking the hired girl, starting breakfast, tending the fire, feeding stock, running the farm in her husband 's absence, which in the aggregate came to ten years.

These were two of the most devoted patriots of their time, sacrificing for their country. "I wonder if future generations will ever know what we have suffered in their behalf," Abigail wrote.

Because schools were closed, she had to educate the children at home. She had to cope with constant shortages and runaway inflation, and somehow hold her own, keep her equilibrium, in the face of the frequent horrors of rampant epidemics, dysentery and smallpox.

At one point she took all of her children, plus a number of her relatives and neighbors, some seventeen people, into

Abigail Adams by Gilbert Stuart

Boston to be inoculated for smallpox. This was a very danger-ous, brave decision, for even if one survived such an ordeal, the misery, the wretched illness that went with it was something nobody would ever wish to experience. And because commu-nication with her husband was so difficult and slow, she had no choice but to make such decisions on her own.

And yet at the close of her long days there on the farm in Braintree, at maybe 10:00 or 11:00 at night, Abigail Adams would sit by the fire at her kitchen table, take up a quill pen, and write some of the most thoughtful, telling letters by any American of the time.

The house is still there. It is the house she lived in as a bride and through all the years of the Revolution when John Adams was off serving the country. Their first son, John Quincy Adams, our sixth president, was born there. And when you go there, you will be moved by how small it is. And how sturdy. Next door is the very similar house where John Adams was born. There they stand, two plain, solid New England salt-boxes by the side of the road. The third Adams house, the much larger Old House, as it's called, is the house John and Abigail moved into after their return from diplomatic service in Europe in 1788.

And then there's the magnificent house they lived in in Paris. There is the house where Adams lived in Amsterdam and in which he very nearly died of fever while securing vitally needed loans from the Dutch during the Revolution.

The house where he and Abigail lived in London, when Adams was our first ambassador to the Court of St. James's, also still stands: the last eighteenth-century house on Grosvenor Square. Talk about buildings redolent with history! Thomas Paine, Thomas Jefferson, Charles Bulfinch, Benjamin West, John Trumbull all came and went.

We can find Adams and Jefferson in Philadelphia still. We can find Adams, Patrick Henry, George Washington, Paul Revere in Carpenters' Hall and in Independence Hall, the Powell House, and old Christ Church. And we can find the Adamses in the White House—they were the first to occupy the White House. All these buildings, these American places, all are tangible, real, evocative expressions of those distant times and those extraordinary people. And those people are here, with us, in a way they would not be if those structures were gone.

Imagine if there were no historic buildings, if there were few or no historic places. Imagine how it would be if there were no Gettysburg battlefield, no Brooklyn Bridge, no Faneuil Hall, no Panama Canal, no Kitty Hawk. The list could be very long. Each and every one could have been swept away, destroyed, heedlessly like so much else.

We Americans say, "What's new?" Nobody ever greets you saying, "What's old?" (Well, maybe preservationists do!)

We think we live in difficult uncertain times. We think we have worries. We think our leaders face difficult decisions. But so it has nearly always been.

When John Adams went off to Philadelphia in 1774, he knew, as the other delegates knew, that only the previous year more than three hundred people had died in the city of smallpox.

Nor was there any certainty of success, or any groundswell of popular support. Had they taken a poll in Philadelphia in 1776, they would have scrapped the whole idea of independence. A third of the country was for it, a third of the country was against it, and the remaining third, in the old human way, was waiting to see who came out on top.

We live in a world where there are twenty cities with populations over ten million people. The entire population of the American colonies was 2,500,000. Philadelphia, the largest American city, had all of thirty thousand people, a small town by our standards.

The same week the Continental Congress voted for independence, the British landed 32,000 troops on Staten Island. In other words, they landed a military force larger than the entire population of our largest city. When the delegates signed their names to that Declaration, pledging "our lives, our fortunes, and our sacred honor," those weren't just words. Each was signing his own death warrant. They were declaring themselves traitors.

One of my favorite of all moments occurred when old Stephen Hopkins, a delegate from Rhode Island, who suffered from palsy, after fixing his spidery signature to the Declaration, remarked, "My hand trembles, but my heart does not."

We've just been through an experience none of us will ever forget. The heartache, the sadness, the grief of September 11 will stay with us as long as we live. I'm sure we all experience that sensation of waking up in the morning, and there's about thirty seconds, maybe a minute, minute and a half, when it's

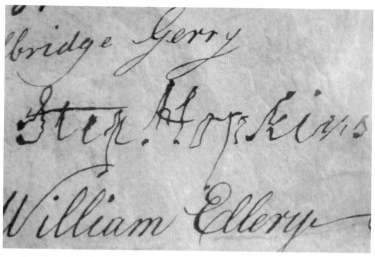

Stephen Hopkins's signature on the Declaration of Independence

not in our minds. And then suddenly it comes back, and we remember.

Because of the magnitude of it, the magnitude of the crime, the magnitude of those buildings coming down before our eyes, dust to dust in an instant, on our own home ground in what we had taken to be peacetime, we will never forget.

It's said that everything has changed. But everything has not changed. This is plain truth. We are still the strongest, most productive, wealthiest, the most creative, the most ingenious, the most generous nation in the world, with the greatest freedoms of any nation in the world, of any nation in all time.

We have resources beyond imagining, and the greatest of these is our brainpower. So far we've not only kept our heads, we're using our heads. And we have much to be proud of since September 11. We have seen a revival of real, genuine patriotism such as we've not seen in our lifetime, or for maybe at least fifty years.

We've seen the most divisive Congress in memory become the most united Congress in memory, for the time being at least. We have all of that to draw upon. And we have a further, all-important, inexhaustible source of strength. And that source of strength is our story, our history, who we are, how we got to be where we are, and all we have been through, what we have achieved.

The Bulwark of Freedom

OHIO UNIVERSITY
Athens, Ohio
2004

For all of us who hold high the value of education and the life of the mind, all who believe our great centers of learning are among the highest, most important attainments of American life, a ceremony such as this is a glorious event. I feel especially honored to take part, as we celebrate both a historic year for Ohio University and a day-of-days for you who are about to receive your degrees.

History is both now and then, today and yesterday. The founding year of this university, 1804, was long ago, and especially as measured by all that has happened over the last two centuries. In 1804, Thomas Jefferson was in the White House.

Lewis and Clark were on their heroic journey. Abraham Lincoln had yet to be born.

All part of the past, we say. No one lived in the past, only the present. You may be interested that the much-used expression "No time like the present" was written in the year 1696.

So here we are on the 12th day of June, in the year 2004, the bicentennial year of Ohio University. At the heart of the university stands Cutler Hall, built in 1816, the oldest building on the campus and an eloquent testament to the vision of the founders.

Now I must tell you that until recently I knew nothing about the Reverend Manasseh Cutler. It was only after receiv-

Cutler Hall, Ohio University

ing Dr. Glidden's invitation that I did my homework, and the more I read the more amazed I was.

As a graduate of Yale University, I was delighted to learn that he was a graduate of Yale. As a resident of Massachusetts, I was pleased to find he lived in Ipswich, north of Boston, where he preached for more than fifty years. Then to my complete surprise, I read that shortly after he was married, he ran a store on the island of Martha's Vineyard, only a few miles from where I live and work.

And just a few days ago my wife and I visited his church and home, both of which still stand.

What a remarkable life he had. He was three doctors in one, doctor of divinity, doctor of law, and a medical doctor, and at one time or other he practiced all three professions. He was, besides, a storekeeper, schoolmaster, army chaplain during the Revolutionary War, congressman, botanist, and astronomer.

Indeed, he seems to have been a university unto himself, and it was he, Manasseh Cutler, who had the vision, as early as 1787, to establish a public university here, the first university west of the Alleghenies.

Physically he was also impressive, tall, massive, and dressed always in ministerial black. But don't picture a somber fellow. He was outgoing, affable, an entertaining storyteller who loved good company and a little politicking. "Social and genial, he was a lover of good cheer . . . a merry laugh was his delight," reads an old account. And fortunately, he was brimming with intellectual curiosity and enterprise.

He was, among other things, the first to attempt a systematic account of the flora of New England. Once, carrying a barometer, he climbed Mount Washington in New Hampshire, New England's highest mountain. But it was when I read that he miscalculated the elevation at the top by no less than 2,600 feet, I felt that here we also have a fellow human being!

Yet for all he packed into one life, nothing compared to his role in the creation of the Northwest Ordinance of 1787.

Think of what that one act of the old Congress—that is the Congress under the Articles of Confederation—brought to pass. Few events in our history have had such far-reaching consequences.

The Northwest Ordinance determined the social, political, and educational institutions for the whole territory that became the five great states of Ohio, Indiana, Illinois, Michigan, and Wisconsin. It provided all the basic rights that were eventually to be guaranteed by the Constitution. Further, it forever prohibited slavery in these states and encouraged public education, and all this as early as 1787.

In language and content, the Northwest Ordinance was very like the constitution of the Commonwealth of Massachusetts, which is the oldest written constitution still in use in the world today. Drafted by John Adams in 1779, during the Revolution, it includes a clause on education unlike any written before. But I will return to that.

The Northwest Ordinance set the standards for five states that comprise in all 260,000 square miles, an area larger than France, five powerhouse states with a combined population today of 45 million people, five states that have come to represent so much that we think of as distinctly, proudly American, from Abraham Lincoln to the Wright brothers, from Cole Porter and Frank Lloyd Wright to John Glenn and Oprah Winfrey, from the hot dog and the automobile to Kellogg's cereal and all but one of the five Great Lakes, not to say a conspicuous wealth of leading colleges and universities.

Imagine, the five states established by the Northwest Ordinance have today a gross national product larger than France, larger than the United Kingdom.

The part the Reverend Cutler played was primarily that of lobbyist. He set off in the early summer of 1787 for New York, to lobby the Congress for the Northwest Ordinance and negotiate the purchase of more than a million acres of land for the new Ohio Company, an enterprise that had been hatched by a number of Revolutionary War veterans in a tavern in Boston. Yes, it all began in a tavern.

It was during his time in New York that the Northwest Ordinance was drafted and passed. The measure of his influence is difficult to determine. But assuredly it was considerable and apparently it was crucial.

It's quite a story. In his diary Reverend Cutler recounts vividly his journey to New York and his time there, giving particular attention to what he ate and the beautiful, accomplished women whose company he enjoyed while campaigning for the grand Ohio project.

Less than a year later, the first settlement was established at Marietta, and the great migration from New England to Ohio was under way. It was called "Ohio Fever." The first wagon bound for Ohio departed from in front of the Reverend Cutler's church on December 3, 1787, as a historic sign there duly proclaims.

Reverend Cutler came to look things over for himself in the summer of 1788. He made the journey from Ipswich to Marietta in a sulky, 751 miles in twenty-nine days, or better than twenty-five miles a day, which back then was top speed.

As an ardent botanist, he gazed in sheer wonder at the trees of Ohio. One black walnut, he recorded, was forty-six feet in circumference.

It was the Reverend Manasseh Cutler who insisted that ample land, the equivalent of two townships, "be given perpetually for the purpose of a university," the historic ground where we are gathered today.

As he wrote later to his son, "It is well known to all concerned with me in transacting the business of the Ohio Company, that the establishment of a university was a first object, and lay with great weight on my mind."

The essence of what is said of knowledge and education in the Northwest Ordinance is also to be found in what John Adams set forth for Massachusetts. The Massachusetts constitution states that "Wisdom and knowledge, as well as virtue, diffused generally among the body of people [are] necessary for the preservation of their rights and liberties." It was the "duty" of the government, Adams wrote, to educate everybody.

The Northwest Ordinance reads, "Religion, morality, and knowledge being necessary to good government and the happiness of mankind, schools and means of education shall be forever encouraged."

These are strong, clear declarations of faith in education as the bulwark of freedom.

For self-government to work, the people must be educated.

To what extent Cutler and Adams compared notes is not easily determined. But they did know one another. They dined together, as Cutler writes in his diary. Cutler was active in the American Academy of Arts and Sciences, which Adams had helped to found. And Cutler is known to have attended the convention in Massachusetts that voted for Adams's constitution.

What the Northwest Ordinance underscores in its clause on education, and Adams did not, is happiness. And this is of greatest importance: Education was seen as the road to happiness, a view with which Adams fervently agreed. They all did in that age of the Enlightenment. Washington, Adams, Jefferson, each in his way made the point, many times. When our founders spoke of the "pursuit of happiness," they did not mean long vacations or the piling up of things.

Happiness was in the enlargement of one's being through the life of the mind and of the spirit. And what was true for the individual was true for a people. Washington, who regretted all his life that he never had the advantage of a formal education, wrote, "Knowledge is in every country the surest basis of public happiness."

Everything was of interest and there was virtually nothing

that could not be learned through a close study of books. That was the creed. "I must judge for myself, but how can I judge, how can any man judge, unless his mind has been opened and enlarged by reading," Adams wrote as a young man. "I cannot live without books," Jefferson famously told Adams in their old age.

Now in the long-standing tradition of commencement speakers, let me offer a few closing thoughts especially for you of the Class of 2004, who are about to set off on your new lives.

- Be glad you're in your shoes.
- We, the older generations, are all for you. You're needed. Your energy, your originality, your idealism are all needed.
- Never forget that one of the greatest of our freedoms is the freedom to think for yourself.
- Read. Read poetry, read biography, read the great literature that has stood the test of time. Read history.
- When bad news is riding high and despair in fashion, when loud mouths and corruption seem to own center stage, when some keep crying that the country is going to the dogs, remember it's always been going to the dogs in the eyes of some, and that 90 percent, or more, of the people are good people, generous-hearted, law-abiding, good citizens who get to work on time, do a

good job, love their country, pay their taxes, care about their neighbors, care about their children's education, and believe, rightly, as you do, in the ideals upon which our way of life is founded.

- See the world. Take up painting. Or the piano. Discover how much you never knew about insects. In the spirit of Manasseh Cutler, go climb a mountain. And skip the barometer.

- Whenever you check out of a hotel or motel, be sure you tip the maid.

Knowing Who We Are

HILLSDALE COLLEGE
Hillsdale, Michigan
2005

Lord Bolingbroke, who was an eighteenth-century political philosopher, called history "philosophy taught with examples." An old friend, the late Daniel Boorstin, who was a very good historian and Librarian of Congress, said that trying to plan for the future without a sense of the past is like trying to plant cut flowers. We're raising a lot of cut flowers and trying to plant them, and that's much of what I want to talk about tonight.

The task of teaching and writing history is infinitely complex and infinitely seductive and rewarding. And it seems to me that one of the truths about history that needs to be made clear to a student or to a reader is that nothing ever had to happen the way it happened. History could have gone off in any number of different directions in any number of different ways at almost any point, just as your own life can. You never know. One thing leads to another. Nothing happens in a vacuum. Actions have consequences. These observations all sound self-evident. But they're not—and particularly to a young person trying to understand life.

And just as we don't know how things are going to turn out for us, those who went before us didn't either. It's all too easy to stand on the mountaintop as a historian or biographer and find fault with people for why they did this or didn't do that, because we're not involved in it, we're not there inside it, we're not confronting what we don't know—as those who preceded us were.

Nor was there ever a self-made man or woman as much as we Americans love that expression. Everyone who's ever lived has been affected, changed, shaped, helped, or hindered by others. We all know, in our own lives, who those people are who've opened a window, given us an idea, given us encouragement, given us a sense of direction, self-approval, self-worth, or who have straightened us out when we were on the wrong path. Most often they have been parents. Almost as often they have been teachers.

Stop and think about those teachers who changed your life, maybe with a single sentence, maybe with one lecture, maybe by just taking an interest in your struggle. Family, teachers, friends, rivals, competitors—they've all shaped us.

And so, too, have people we've never met, never known, because they lived long before us. They, too, have shaped us— they who composed the music that moves us, the painters, the poets, those who have written the great literature in our language. We walk around every day, every one of us, quoting Shakespeare, Cervantes, Pope. We don't know it, but we are, all the time. We think this is our way of speaking. It isn't our way of speaking—it's what we have been given.

The laws we live by, the freedoms we enjoy, the institutions that we take for granted—and we should never take for granted—are all the work of others who went before us. And to be indifferent to that isn't just to be ignorant, it's to be rude. And ingratitude is a shabby failing.

How can we not want to know about the people who have made it possible for us to live as we live, to have the freedoms we have, to be citizens of this greatest of countries? It's not just a birthright, it is something that others struggled and strived for, often suffered for, often were defeated for and died for, for the next generation, for us.

Now, those who wrote and signed their names to the Declaration of Independence that fateful summer of 1776 were by no means superhuman. Every single one had his flaws, his weaknesses. Some of them ardently disliked others of them. Each did things in life he regretted. But the fact that they could rise to the occasion as they did, these imperfect human beings, and do what they did is also, of course, a testimony to their humanity.

We are not just known by our failings, by our weaknesses,

by our sins. We are known by being capable of rising to the occasion with the courage of our convictions.

The Greeks said that character is destiny, and the more I read of the human story, the more convinced I am they were right. You look at the great portraits by John Trumbull or Charles Willson Peale or John Singleton Copley or Gilbert Stuart of those remarkable leaders present at the creation of our nation, you realize they aren't just likenesses. They are delineations of character and were intended to be. And we need to understand that they, the founders, knew that what they had created was no more perfect than they were. And that this has been to our advantage. It has been good that it wasn't all just handed to us in perfect condition, all ready to run smoothly in perpetuity—that it needed to be constantly attended to and improved and made to work better.

I have just returned from a cruise through the Panama Canal. I think often about why the French failed at Panama and why we succeeded. One of the reasons is that we were attuned to adaptation, to doing what works, whereas the French engineers were trained to do everything in a certain way. We Americans have a gift for improvisation. We improvise in jazz; we improvise in many of our architectural breakthroughs. Improvisation is one of our traits, as a people, because it was essential, it was necessary, because again and again and again we were attempting what hadn't been done before.

Keep in mind that when we were founded by those Americans of the eighteenth century, none had had any prior experience in revolutions or nation making. They were, as we would say, winging it. They were idealistic and they were young. We see their faces in the old paintings done later in their lives or looking at us from the paper money in our wallets, and we see the awkward teeth and the powdered hair, and we think of them as elder statesmen. But George Washington, when he took command of the Continental Army at Cambridge in 1775, was forty-three, and he was the oldest of them. Jefferson was thirty-three when he wrote the Declaration of Independence. John Adams was forty. Benjamin Rush—one of the most interesting of them all—was thirty when he signed the Declaration.

They were young people, feeling their way, improvising, trying to do what would work. They had no money, no navy, no real army. There wasn't a bank in the entire country. It was a country of just 2,500,000 people, 500,000 of whom were held in slavery.

And think of this: Few nations in the world know when they were born. We know exactly when we began and why we began and who did it.

In the Rotunda of the Capitol in Washington hangs John Trumbull's great painting *The Declaration of Independence*. It's our best-known scene from our past. And almost nothing about it is accurate. The Declaration of Independence wasn't signed on July 4. They didn't start to sign the Declaration until August 2, and only a part of the Congress was then present. The rest would be coming back for months to follow to take their turn signing.

The Declaration of Independence by John Trumbull

The chairs in the painting are wrong, the doors are in the wrong place. There were no heavy draperies at the windows, as in the painting, and the display of military flags and banners on the back wall is strictly a figment of Trumbull's imagination.

What is accurate are the faces. Each and every one of the forty-seven men in that painting is an identifiable—and thus accountable—individual. We know what they look like. We know who they were. And that's what Trumbull wanted. He wanted us to know them and not forget them. Because this momentous step wasn't a proclamation being handed down by a potentate or a king or a czar. It was the decision of a Congress acting freely.

Unfortunately, we are raising a generation of young Americans who are by and large historically illiterate. Innumerable studies have been made and there's no denying it. I've experienced it myself again and again. I had a young woman come up to me after a talk I had given at a college in Missouri to thank me for coming to the campus, because, she said, "until now I never understood that the original thirteen colonies were all on the East Coast."

Now you hear that and you think: What in the world have we done? How could this fine young American, a student at a good college, not know that?

I taught a seminar at one of our Ivy League colleges of twenty-five seniors, all majoring in history, all honor students. The first morning we met, to get things going, I asked, "How many of you know who George C. Marshall was?"

Not one. There was a long silence. Finally one young man asked, "Did he maybe have something to do with the Marshall Plan?" And I said yes, he certainly did, and that was a good way to begin talking about George Marshall.

We have to do several things. First of all we have to get across the idea that we have to know who we were if we're to know who we are and where we're headed. This is essential. We have to value what our forebears—and not just in the eighteenth century, but our own parents and grandparents— did for us, or we're not going to take it very seriously, and it can slip away. If you don't care about it—if you've inherited some great work of art that is worth a fortune and you don't know that it's worth a fortune, you don't even know that it's a great work of art and you're not interested in it—you're going to lose it.

We have to do a far better job of teaching our teachers. The great teachers—the teachers who influence you, who change your lives—almost always, I'm sure, are the teachers who love what they are teaching. It is that wonderful teacher who says, "Come over here and look in this microscope, you're really going to get a kick out of this."

There was a wonderful professor of child psychology at the University of Pittsburgh named Margaret McFarland. I wish her ideas were better known. She said that attitudes aren't taught, they're caught. If the teacher has enthusiasm for the subject at hand, the student catches that, be it in second grade or graduate school. She said, "Show them what you love."

Also, if the teachers know what they are teaching, they are much less dependent on textbooks. I don't know when you last picked up an American history textbook. There are, to be sure, some very good ones. But most, it would seem, have been created in order to kill any interest one might have in history.

I've had the thought that students might be better served if the teacher were to cut out all the pages, clip off the page numbers, then mix them all up and ask the student to put it all back together in the right order. Too many of the textbooks are dreary, done by committee, often hilariously politically correct. Students should not have to read anything that we wouldn't want to read ourselves. And there are wonderful books, past and present. There is literature in history—Longfellow, for example, Lincoln's Second Inaugural Address, the speeches of Martin Luther King.

History isn't just something that ought to be taught, read,

or encouraged only because it will make us better citizens. It will make us a better citizen and it will make us more thoughtful and understanding human beings. It should be taught for the pleasure it provides. The pleasure of history, like art or music or literature, consists in an expansion of the experience of being alive, which, indeed, is what education is largely about.

And we need not leave the whole job of teaching history to the teachers. If I could have you come away from what I have to say tonight remembering one thing, it would be this: The teaching of history, the emphasis on the importance of history, the enjoyment of history, should begin at home.

We who are parents or grandparents should be taking our children to historic sites. We should be talking about those books in biography or history that we have particularly enjoyed, or those characters in history who have meant something to us. We should be talking about what it was like when we were growing up in the olden days. Children, particularly young children, love this. And in my view, the real focus should be at the grade-school level. We all know that those young children can learn languages so fast it takes your breath away. The fact is they can learn *anything* so fast it takes your breath away. And the truth is they *want* to learn. They can be taught to dissect a cow's eye. They can be taught anything.

There's no great secret to teaching history or to making history interesting. Barbara Tuchman said it in two words, "Tell stories." That's what history is: story.

And what's a story? E. M. Forster gave a wonderful definition to it: If I say to you the king died and then the queen died, that's a sequence of events. If I say the king died and the queen died of grief, that's a story. That's human. That calls for empathy on the part of the teller of the story and of the reader or listener to the story.

We ought to be growing, encouraging, developing historians who have heart and empathy enough to put students in the time and circumstances of those before us who were just as human and real as we are.

We've got to teach history and nurture history and encourage history because it's an antidote to the hubris of the present—the idea that everything we have and everything we do and everything we think is the ultimate, the best.

We should never look down on those of the past and say they should have known better. What do you think they will be saying about us in the future? They're going to be saying *we* should have known better. Why in the world did we do that? What could we have been thinking?

Samuel Eliot Morison said we ought to read history because it will help us to behave better. It does. And we ought to read history because it helps to break down the dividers between the disciplines of science, medicine, philosophy, art, music. It's all part of the human story and ought to be seen as such. You can't understand it unless you see it that way. You can't understand the eighteenth century, for example, unless you understand the vocabulary of the eighteenth century. What did they mean by those words?

There's a line in one of the letters written by John Adams

where he's telling his wife, Abigail, at home, "We can't guarantee success [in this war] but we can do something better. We can deserve it." Think how different that is from the attitude today when all that matters for far too many is success, being number one, getting ahead, getting to the top. However you betray or claw or cheat is immaterial if you get to the top.

That line in the Adams letter is saying that how the War for Independence turns out is in the hands of God. We can't control that, but we can control how we behave. We can deserve success. When I read that line while doing research for my book on John Adams, it practically lifted me out of my chair. Then about three weeks later I was reading some correspondence written by George Washington and there was the very same line. I thought, wait a minute, what's going on? They must be quoting something. So, I got down *Bartlett's Familiar Quotations*, and started going through the entries from the eighteenth century and there it was! The line is from the play *Cato* by Joseph Addison. They were quoting something from the literature of the time, scripture of a kind, a kind of secular creed if you will. And we can't fully understand why they behaved as they did then if we don't understand that. We can't understand why honor was so important to them and why they were truly ready to put their lives, their fortunes, their sacred honor on the line. Those weren't just words.

I want to read to you a letter young John Quincy Adams received from his mother. The boy was being taken across the North Atlantic in the midst of winter, in the midst of war. Just outside Boston Harbor British ships were waiting to capture somebody like John Adams and take him to London, where most likely he would be hanged as a traitor. But the boy went, too, his mother knowing that she probably wouldn't see him again for a year or more, maybe never.

Why? Because she and his father wanted John Quincy to be in association with Franklin and the great political philosophers of France, to learn to speak French, to travel in Europe, to be able to soak it all up. And they risked his life for that—for his education.

We have little idea of what people were willing to do for education in times past. It's the one sustaining theme through our whole history—that the next generation will be better educated than we are. John Adams himself was a living example of the transforming miracle of education. His father was able to write his name, we know. His mother was almost certainly illiterate. But because he had a scholarship to Harvard, everything changed for him. As he said, "I discovered books and read forever," and he did. And he and Abigail wanted this for their son no less.

It was a horrendous voyage. Everything that could have gone wrong, went wrong. And when the boy came back, he said he didn't ever want to go across the Atlantic again as long as he lived. And then his father was called back, and his mother said you're going back. And here is what she wrote to him. And please keep in mind this is being written to an eleven-year-old boy and listen to how different it is from how we talk to our children in our time. It's as if she were addressing a grown-up. She's talking to someone they want to bring along quickly because there's work to do and survival is essential:

> *These are the times in which a genius would wish to live. It is not in the still calm of life or the repose of a pacific station that great characters are formed. The habits of a vigorous mind are formed in contending with difficulties. Great necessities call out great virtues. When a mind is raised and animated by scenes that engage the heart, then those qualities which would otherwise lay dormant wake into life and form the character of the hero and the statesman.*

Now, there are several interesting things going on in that letter. For all the times that she mentions the mind, in the last sentence she says, "When a mind is raised and animated by scenes that engage the heart, then those qualities which would otherwise lay dormant wake into life and form the character of the hero and the statesman." In other words, the mind itself isn't enough. You have to have the heart.

Well, of course he went and the history of our country is different because of it. John Quincy Adams, in my view, was the most superbly educated and maybe the most brilliant human being who ever occupied the executive office. He was a great secretary of state—he wrote the Monroe Doctrine, among other things—and he was a wonderful human being and a great writer. Told to keep a diary by his father when he was in Europe, he kept the diary for sixty-five years. And the diaries are extraordinary, essays on all manner of subjects.

After the war was over, Abigail went to Europe to be with her husband when he became our first minister to the Court of St. James's. And John Quincy came home from Europe to prepare for Harvard. And he had not been home in Massachusetts very long when Abigail received a letter from her sister saying that John Quincy was a very impressive young man—and that of course everybody was quite astonished that he could speak French—but, alas, he seemed overly enamored with himself and with his own opinions and that this was not going over very well in town. So Abigail sat down in a house that still stands on Grosvenor Square in London and wrote a letter to John Quincy. And here's what she said:

> *If you are conscious to yourself that you possess more knowledge upon some subjects than others of your standing, reflect that you have had greater opportunities of seeing the world and obtaining knowledge of mankind than any of your contemporaries. That you have never wanted a book, but it has been supplied to you. That your whole time has been spent in the company of men of literature and science. How unpardonable would it have been in you to have turned out a blockhead.*

How unpardonable it would be for us—with so much that we have been given, the advantages we have, all the continuing opportunities we have to enhance and increase our love of learning—to turn out blockheads. Or to raise blockheads.

What we do in education, what these wonderful teachers and administrators and college presidents and college and university trustees do is the best, most important work there is.

So I salute you all for your interest in education and in the education of Hillsdale. I salute you for coming out tonight to be at an event like this. Not just sitting at home being a spectator. It's important that we take part. Citizenship isn't just voting. We all know that. Let's all pitch in. And never lose heart.

The Ties That Bind

THE 250TH BIRTHDAY OF
THE MARQUIS DE LAFAYETTE
LAFAYETTE COLLEGE

Easton, Pennsylvania

2007

The triumphal return of the Marquis de Lafayette to America in the year 1824 produced a public outpouring of goodwill and gratitude across the nation unlike that ever inspired by a visitor from abroad, before or since. The grand tour that began with his arrival at New York on August 16, covered all twenty-four states of the Union and went on for thirteen months. The country had never experienced anything like it. Everywhere Lafayette was greeted with huge, unprecedented, wildly enthusiastic crowds. "All through this trip," he wrote,

Marquis de Lafayette by Samuel F. B. Morse

"we have felt everything which can touch or flatter the human heart." When the mayor of a little town near Boston told him, "Sir, America loves you," Lafayette replied, "Sir, I truly love America," and no one doubted he meant every word.

He traveled more than six thousand miles, as far north as Burlington, Vermont, west as far as St. Louis, south all the way to New Orleans. He traveled the Mississippi River, the Ohio, the new Erie Canal. He saw Niagara Falls. He was Jefferson's guest at Monticello and visited Andrew Jackson at the Hermitage. At Mount Vernon, in one of the most moving moments of the odyssey, he paid homage at the tomb of George Washington. Daniel Webster delivered the welcoming oration at ceremonies at Bunker Hill.

He visited Harvard, Yale, and Princeton. Dedicating a library at Brooklyn, he paused to bestow a kiss on a little boy who happened to be Walt Whitman. At Philadelphia, Independence Hall, which had fallen into shameful decay, was resuscitated and thus saved, in order to provide the famous guest a fitting place to greet his adoring public.

He was hailed as the last remaining general of the Continental Army and "the venerable symbol of a past heroic age." One contemporary account after another describes the resplendent triumphal arches erected, the parades and elegant carriages drawn by white horses, banners and flags flying, cannon booming, dinners and dancing and choral oratorios, and crowds such as no one had ever seen. And Lafayette, though old and lame, thrived on it. Indeed, by all appearances, it was the happiest he had ever been. As Jefferson noted, the illustrious Frenchman had "a canine appetite for popularity and fame."

Though the so-called Era of Good Feeling under President James Monroe was, like Monroe's time in office, drawing to a close, and there were issues of insistent, troubling kinds manifesting themselves—the extension of slavery being not the least of them—the mood of the country overall was confident, optimistic. Signs of material progress were plain to be seen on all sides, as countless speakers, including Lafayette, made a great point of.

Above all, the show of gratitude was both resonant and genuine—gratitude not only for the heroic part Lafayette had played in the struggle for American independence, but for those of the whole founding generation of Americans who had made possible the blessings and unparalleled opportunities of the new nation.

Moreover, the yearlong pageantry marked a celebratory start to what would prove down the years an extraordinary relationship between France and the United States, which, if not always smooth or easy, was nonetheless like that we have known with no other country, and of greater, more lasting benefit than is commonly appreciated. And this was all the more remarkable given that France, let us remember, had been our first enemy, during the French and Indian War, and only a scant decade or so before the start of the American Revolution.

It was well into the Revolutionary War before we and the French became allies. That was agreed to formally early in

1778 in Paris and it was one of the most fateful agreements in our history. The young Lafayette, meanwhile, had arrived on our shores at age nineteen to offer his services as a soldier in the Glorious Cause of America and to earn his place as a full-fledged American hero.

Perhaps we could have won the Revolutionary War without help from France, perhaps not. There is no clear answer. But certainly we would not have succeeded when we did had it not been for the French. As too few Americans seem to understand, the French troops under Rochambeau at Yorktown, the last great battle of the war, numbered more than our own forces under Washington, and it was the arrival of the French fleet at exactly the right time off the Virginia Peninsula that left Cornwallis no choice but to surrender.

It was again in Paris that the treaty was signed ending the war—the all-important treaty in which His Britannic Majesty George III recognized the United States to be "free, sovereign, and independent states." A plaque on the white wall of the old Hôtel d'York on rue Jacob marks the spot.

American history was made that day in Paris, September 3, 1783. The new independent United States of America had arrived on the world stage. And in the time since, more American history has unfolded in France than in any country other than our own.

Benjamin Franklin and John Adams, having served all-important diplomatic roles in Paris during the war, and in the negotiations that ended it, were afterward joined by Thomas Jefferson, who was to stay on in Paris as our minister to France for five years—five of the happiest years of Jefferson's life.

During World War I more than two million American soldiers served "over there." (Contrary to popular understanding, the famous line, "Lafayette, we are here," was not delivered by General Pershing on his arrival, but by Colonel Charles Stanton at a ceremony at Lafayette's grave.) Nearly 80,000 Americans died in France in World War I. During World War II another generation of American soldiers, in all 790,000, served in France, and more than 57,000 died there.

France is truly hallowed ground for Americans, let us always remember. Of the American dead from both wars more than 60,000 are buried in French soil, at Meuse-Argonne, Normandy, and four other cemeteries. At Meuse-Argonne, the largest, lie fully 41,246 American dead.

Charles de Gaulle and Dwight Eisenhower, Paris, 1944

It was also in France—in Paris close by the Place de la Concorde—that headquarters for the Marshall Plan was established in 1950.

Much of this is familiar history, I know. But some things bear repeating. As Samuel Johnson wrote, we "more frequently require to be reminded than informed." Besides, there is far more to history than wars and foreign affairs, and that, too, must be taken into account in any fair appreciation of the ties that bind America and France.

The love of Paris by talented, aspiring young Americans, its large importance as a place of inspiration and creative freedom, dates from our very beginnings as a country. Time and again Paris changed their lives and thus hugely influenced American art, American literature, music, dance, and yes, American science, technology, and medicine.

It was in Paris in 1784, in the library of Jefferson's mansion on the Champs-Élysées, that Jefferson and the young American artist John Trumbull blocked out on a small sheet of paper the idea for Trumbull's famous portrayal of the signing of the Declaration of Independence, the painting which, over time, has been seen by more people than any ever done by an American. And it was there in Paris that Trumbull, ambitious to make a mark and encouraged by Jefferson, embarked on the series of historic portraits and paintings of the Revolution that were to be his great life works.

John Singleton Copley, another of the eighteenth-century American masters, wrote of "something in the air" in Paris that quickened creative vitality. James McNeill Whistler, who arrived in Paris in the 1850s, unknown, penniless, and precocious, would all but reinvent himself there. Mary Cassatt from Philadelphia, settling in Paris in 1877, felt she could at long last work with total independence. "I began to live," she wrote.

Paris was the capital of the art world, the Louvre, its Pantheon, and the legion of aspiring Americans who flocked to the city to paint, sculpt, study, to live the *vie de bohème* reads like a Who's Who of American Art—Trumbull, Copley, Samuel F. B. Morse, Whistler, Mary Cassatt, John Singer Sargent, Winslow Homer, Thomas Eakins, Henry Tanner, Augustus Saint-Gaudens, Childe Hassam, to name only a few.

Samuel F. B. Morse spent the better part of his time in Paris, during the early 1830s, painting a huge interior view of the grand gallery at the Louvre. Earlier, while Lafayette was in New York, Morse had been chosen to do the French hero's portrait, a dramatic, life-size painting that hangs still in New York's City Hall. It was later, on his voyage home, inspired by something he'd seen in France, that Morse conceived the fundamental idea for the telegraph.

John Singer Sargent was an immediate triumph. His *Madame X*, the portrait of Madame Pierre Gautreau that caused a sensation in Paris, was done when Sargent was all of twenty-eight.

Inspired by French Impressionists, Americans by the dozens became Impressionists. Childe Hassam learned to paint as readily with the fluid brushwork of the French Impressionists April showers on the Champs-Élysées as he would an October morning on Beacon Street, Boston, or Fifth Avenue with all flags flying on Allies Day, 1917.

Those artists who didn't get to Paris wished they could. And the pull for writers was no less. Some of the greatest landmarks in American literature—works as thoroughly American as any we have—were, in fact, written under the spell of Paris, "the light of Paris . . . the far spreading presence of Paris," as Henry James wrote.

I have fallen in love with American names,
The sharp names that never get flat,
The snake-skin title of mining claims,
The plumed war-bonnet of Medicine Hat,
Tucson and Deadwood and Lost Mule Flat.

These, the wonderful opening lines of Stephen Vincent Benét's poem "American Names," were composed not, as one might assume, somewhere west of the Brazos, but in Paris. And so, too, was Benét's great narrative poem of the Civil War, *John Brown's Body.*

Ralph Waldo Emerson, recalling his own time in Paris, a generation earlier, had observed, "We go to Europe to be Americanized."

No less an American classic than James Fenimore Cooper's

The Prairie was written during the seven years Cooper made Paris his home. *Ethan Frome—Ethan Frome* of all books!— was written in the library of Edith Wharton's sumptuous apartment on the rue de Varenne in 1911, in the heyday of the Belle Époque or about as far removed from the bleak New England setting of her classic novel as one could imagine. In fact, her story had its origins in French, as an exercise done for her French teacher in Paris.

In the New York society of her childhood, as Edith Wharton recounts in her autobiography, the arts were a world apart. Her mother and father considered authorship in particular as "something between a black art and common labor," and certainly not for her. In Paris, as nowhere else, she wrote, her work became "the core" of her life. With the outbreak of World War I, she was one of the first American women to volunteer in the French war effort, collecting clothing, food, and medical supplies. By the time the war was over, 25,000 American women served in France, a point of history too little known or appreciated on both sides of the Atlantic. Among those men and women who came home from the war were a substantial, though unknowable, number whose outlook was no longer the same, as expressed by the popular song of the day: "How Ya Gonna Keep 'Em Down on the Farm After They've Seen Paree?"

In the decades after the war, an estimated 35,000 Americans took up life in Paris. It was the place to be, and especially for the young, the gifted, and aspiring. "I arrived fresh out of Brooklyn, twenty, and all agog," remembered Aaron Copland.

Gertrude Stein and Ernest Hemingway, the two outstanding self-promoters of the day, made famous "their" Paris of the 1920s, but, of course, there were hundreds of others writing, painting, composing music, experimenting with modern dance, or just soaking up the expatriate life. You know them: William Faulkner, F. Scott Fitzgerald, Grant Wood, Edward Hopper, Richard Wright, Langston Hughes, Sherwood Anderson, Stephen Vincent Benét, Carson McCullers, Hart Crane, Cole Porter, George Gershwin, Isadora Duncan, Josephine Baker.

Langston Hughes

Like their counterparts of an earlier time, they found a kind of spiritual home in France and among the French. Especially for creative, independent-minded American women and for African Americans like Richard Wright, Langston Hughes, and Josephine Baker, there was freedom of a kind, an acceptance, such as they had not known in their own country.

It's a matter of no small importance that in the era before World War I, the two outstanding American women in art and literature—two who hold an enduring place in the forefront among all American painters and writers—Mary Cassatt and Edith Wharton, could only find themselves and thrive in their work as they did far from America, in Paris, and yet they never considered themselves as anything other than Americans. Mary Cassatt lived out her long life in Paris and is buried there. Edith Wharton, too, except for summers in Massachusetts, made Paris her home and is buried there, as are Isadora Duncan and Josephine Baker. The funeral service for dancer Josephine Baker at the Church of the Madeleine in 1975 was the grandest Paris funeral ever seen for an American.

Cole Porter, back from years in France, set his last two Broadway musicals, *Can-Can* and *Silk Stockings*, in Paris. He was old and ill when he wrote the song "I Love Paris," but as William Zinsser has said, it "still sounds young and enamored of the city in every season and every kind of weather, from drizzle to sizzle."

It was in the antique shops of Paris that George Gershwin found the taxi horns with exactly the sound he needed for his *American in Paris* suite. Years after Gershwin's death, the 1951 movie *An American in Paris*, with an all-Gershwin score and starring Gene Kelly, became a tremendous hit and won six Oscars, including Best Picture. An enduring classic, it gave millions of Americans a feeling for Paris they would never quite lose.

(I must tell you that as an impressionable eighteen-year-old college freshman from Pittsburgh who was head over heels in

George Gershwin

love at the time and dreaming of becoming an artist, to see Gene Kelly—who came from Pittsburgh—up there on the big screen unabashedly in love, dancing, singing, and painting his way through Paris to his heart's delight . . . Well, that was something!)

John Adams and Thomas Jefferson are both on record that after their own country, they would have chosen first to live in France. But as an example of a skeptical, disapproving American changing her tune, none surpasses Abigail Adams, who at first found almost nothing to like about Paris or the French. The dirt, the morals, the extravagances and frivolities were by her starch Yankee standards perfectly deplorable. Yet in less than a year, when it came time to go, she hated to leave. She spoke no French, as her husband and her son John Quincy did. That hardly mattered. She had been completely won over. She loved the opera, the theater, the acceptance of women in polite circles as the social and intellectual equals of men. In young Madame de Lafayette she had found one of the warmest friendships of her lifetime. Adrienne de Lafayette was still in her twenties. She spoke English and despite her wealth and position, dressed simply and disliked pretentious display quite as much as did Abigail Adams. She was, as well, like Abigail, openly devoted to her husband and children.

At the Massachusetts Historical Society in Boston are the letters of John and Abigail Adams dating from their time in

Paris, as well as Jefferson's Paris love letters to the English artist Maria Cosway, and the original manuscript of the only book Jefferson ever wrote, his *Notes on the State of Virginia*, which was first published in France. And there, too, are letters from Paris by Dr. John Collins Warren, the Boston surgeon who famously demonstrated ether anesthesia for the first time, these written in the early nineteenth century when Paris was considered the leading center for medical studies and advanced medical practice, and Dr. Warren was an intensely serious student there. Oliver Wendell Holmes, Sr., is another who studied medicine in Paris, and his letters, written in the 1830s, are among the most engaging we have. Dr. Holmes, famous as the author of *The Autocrat of the Breakfast-Table*, taught anatomy at Harvard for thirty-five years, his influence reaching far.

But think, too, of the famous landmarks and monuments here in America that we consider so very American, so emblematic of American greatness, American freedoms, enterprise, or ingenuity, and that are, in fact, French in part or whole. Our capital city on the Potomac was laid out by the French architect and engineer Major Pierre L'Enfant. The magnificent life-size statue of George Washington at the state capitol of Virginia in Richmond—the great prototype for nearly every American sculpture of Washington—is the work of the French master Jean-Antoine Houdon. Jefferson's Monticello, with its picturesque dome, is a French house in spirit and in detail, inspired by a Paris landmark, the Hôtel de Salm, a building Jefferson adored and that still stands beside the Seine.

The Louisiana Purchase pretty much fell into our lap when Napoleon offered it to Jefferson at a bargain price. Yet, the fact remains that the geographic reach of the United States of America thus more than doubled with the acquisition of land that had belonged to France.

And certainly at a gathering such as this we should not forget the master work of the French historian Alexis de Tocqueville, *Democracy in America*. Published in 1835, it remains one of the wisest books ever written about us.

The Brooklyn Bridge owes the very legs it stands on to the pioneering work of French civil engineers. (Its ingenious underwater foundations were worked out by Washington Roebling from studies he made in France of "caissons" first developed by the French.) And it was the brilliant French engineer Baron Godin de Lépinay who saw as no one did, the only way to succeed with a ship canal across Panama. His plan, presented at an international conference on the Left Bank in Paris in 1879, and roundly ridiculed by French and American engineers alike, is the Panama Canal of today, our "American triumph."

Then, to be sure, there is our surpassing gift from France, Miss Liberty herself, holding high the beacon of freedom in New York Harbor. No other country ever honored another with a gift of such magnitude or everlasting popularity.

And think of all the places on the map of America besides Louisiana and New Orleans and Baton Rouge—the cities, states, small towns, lakes, and rivers—that have names that are entirely French, however badly we pronounce them:

Statue of Liberty torch

Des Moines, Lake Champlain, St. Louis, Sault Ste. Marie, Terre Haute, Vermont. And all those American colleges and universities called Duquesne, Marquette, Notre Dame, and, yes indeed, Lafayette.

We Americans love French fashions, French lace, French doors, French dressing. We've made French fries a national staple. We celebrate all out with French champagne, gussy up with French perfume and French cuffs, and call it "puttin' on the Ritz"—as at the Ritz *in Paris*, that is. On evenings like this, if the speaker runs on too long, you are perfectly within your rights to consider French leave.

For all our love of French wine, and as dearly as we pay for the pleasure, it represents a mere 3 percent of all that we import from France. What we buy most from France are machinery, construction materials, and airplanes. Further, the United States has become the largest investor in France. France is the travel destination of choice for two million Americans a year, and once there we stay longer than anyone. Meanwhile some 1,300,000 of our students are taking French, making it, after Spanish, the second most commonly studied foreign language.

When considering Americans of French descent worth noting, we might start with Paul Revere. In all, eleven million of us claim French or French Canadian descent.

The one serious breach with France in our early years as a nation was the undeclared war at sea during the presidency of

John Adams. And extremely serious it was. Then, during negotiations to resolve the crisis, came the odorous XYZ Affair. It very nearly turned into a full-scale war with Napoleon, but to the everlasting credit of John Adams and his chief emissary to France, John Marshall, an honorable settlement was reached. For Adams it was the proudest, most beneficial accomplishment of his presidency. As he would tell a friend, "I desire no other inscription over my gravestone than: 'Here lies John Adams, who took upon himself the responsibility of peace with France in the year 1800.'"

Adams lived to see Lafayette's return in 1824 and there was a moving reunion of the two old patriots, when Lafayette paid a call at Quincy.

As a gesture of national gratitude Congress awarded Lafayette, who was deeply in debt, a cash grant of $250,000, an absolute fortune and approximately what he had earlier contributed from his own funds to help the cause of the American Revolution. The day of Lafayette's departure from Washington, in 1825, after a long visit at the White House, the new president, John Quincy Adams, his voice trembling, spoke for all the American people. Here is what he said:

> *We shall look upon you always as belonging to us, during the whole of a life, as belonging to our children after us. You are ours by more than patriotic self-devotion with which you flew to the aid of our fathers at the crisis of our fate, ours by that unshaken gratitude for your services which is a precious portion of our inheritance, ours*

by that tie of love, stronger than death, which has linked
your name for endless ages of time with the name Wash-
ington. . . . Speaking in the name of the whole people of
the United States and at a loss only for language to give
utterance to that feeling of attachment with which the
heart of the nation beats as the heart of one man—I bid
you a reluctant and affectionate farewell.

On this occasion, gathered as we are here to honor Lafayette
in our way, let us wish wholeheartedly that the ties that bind
America and France, and the tradition of respect and affection
between our countries, will continue with renewed spirit.

The Love of Learning

BOSTON COLLEGE

Boston, Massachusetts

2008

We haven't a lot of ceremony left in American life, alas, but commencements do go on, year after year, and in the grand tradition, with full, appropriate panoply, bringing together, as we see here today, people from all walks of life, all parts of the country, and indeed of the world, to pay tribute to genuinely worthy accomplishment. The importance of education has been a prevailing theme in American life from the beginning and may it ever be so.

Information. Information at our fingertips. Information without end . . .

The Library of Congress has 650 miles of shelves and books in 470 languages . . . Napoleon was afraid of cats . . . A porcupine is born with 30,000 quills . . . A mosquito beats its wings 600 times per second . . . Coal production in the United States is second only to that of China . . .

It's said ad infinitum: Ours is the Information Age. There's never been anything like it since the dawn of creation. We glory in the Information Highway as other eras gloried in railroads. Information for all! Information night and day!

. . . A column of air a mile square, starting 50 feet from the ground and extending to 14,000 feet contains an average of 25,000,000 insects . . . James Madison weighed less than 100 pounds, William Howard Taft, 332 pounds, a presidential record . . . According to the *World Almanac*, the length of the index finger on the Statue of Liberty is 8 feet . . . The elevation of the highest mountain in Massachusetts, Mount Greylock, is 3,487 feet . . . The most ancient living tree in America, a bristlecone pine in California, is 4,700 years old . . .

Information is useful. Information is often highly interesting. Information has value, sometimes great value. The right bit of information at the opportune moment can be worth a fortune. Information can save time and effort. Information can save your life. The value of information, facts, figures, and the like, depends on what we make of it—on *judgment*.

But information, let us be clear, isn't learning. Information isn't poetry. Or art. Or Gershwin or the Shaw Memorial. Or faith. It isn't wisdom.

Facts alone are never enough. Facts rarely if ever have any soul. In writing or trying to understand history one may have all manner of "data" and miss the point. One can have all the facts and miss the truth. It can be like the old piano teacher's lament to her student, "I hear all the notes, but I hear no music."

If information were learning, you could memorize the *World Almanac* and call yourself educated. If you memorized the *World Almanac*, you wouldn't be educated. You'd be weird!

Learning is not to be found on a printout. It's not on call at the touch of the finger. Learning is acquired mainly from books, and most readily from great books. And from teachers, and the more learned and empathetic the better. And from work, concentrated work.

Abigail Adams put it perfectly more than two hundred years ago: "Learning is not attained by chance. It must be sought with ardor and attended with diligence." *Ardor*, to my mind, is the key word.

For many of you of the graduating class, the love of learning has already taken hold. For others it often happens later and often by surprise, as history has shown time and again. That's part of the magic.

Consider the example of Charles Sumner, the great Senator Charles Sumner of Massachusetts, whose statue stands in the Boston Public Garden facing Boylston Street.

Charles Sumner

As a boy in school Charles Sumner had shown no particular promise. Nor did he distinguish himself as an undergraduate at Harvard. He did love reading, however, and by the time he finished law school, something overcame him. Passionate to know more, learn more, he put aside the beginnings of a law practice and sailed for France on his own and on borrowed money, in order to attend lectures at the Sorbonne. It was a noble adventure in independent scholarship, if ever there was.

Everything was of interest to him. He attended lectures on natural history, geology, Egyptology, criminal law, the history of philosophy, and pursued a schedule of classical studies that would have gladdened the heart of the legendary Father Thayer of Boston College. He attended lectures at the Paris medical schools. He went to the opera, the theater, the Louvre, all the while pouring out his excitement in the pages of his journal and in long letters home. Trying to express what he felt on seeing the works of Raphael and Leonardo da Vinci at the Louvre, he wrote, "They touched my mind, untutored as it is, like a rich strain of music."

But there was more. Something else touched him deeply. At lectures at the Sorbonne he had observed how black students were perfectly at ease with and well received by the other students. The color of one's skin seemed to make no difference. Sumner was pleased to see this, though at first it struck him as strange. But then he thought, as he wrote, that maybe the "distance" between blacks and whites at home was something white Americans had been taught and that "does not exist in the nature of things." And therein was the seed from which would later arise, in the 1850s, before the Civil War, Charles Sumner's strident stand on the floor of the United States Senate against the spread of slavery. From his quest for learning he brought home a personal revelation he had not anticipated and it changed history.

When I set out to write the life of John Adams, I wanted not only to read what he and Abigail wrote, but to read as much as possible of what they read. We're all what we read to a very considerable degree.

So there I was past age sixty taking up once again, for the first time since high school and college English classes, the essays of Samuel Johnson and works of Pope, Swift, and Laurence Sterne. I read Samuel Richardson's *Clarissa*, which was Abigail's favorite novel; and Cervantes—*Don Quixote*—for the first time in my life. What a joy!

Cervantes is part of us, whether we know it or not. Declare you're in a pickle; talk of birds of a feather flocking together; vow to turn over a new leaf; give the devil his due;

Miguel de Cervantes

or insist that mum's the word, and you're quoting Cervantes every time.

John Adams read everything—Shakespeare and the Bible over and over, and the Psalms especially. He read poetry, fiction, history. Always carry a book with you on your travels he advised his son John Quincy. "You will never be alone with a poet in your pocket." In a single year, according to the U.S. Department of Education, among all Americans with a college education, fully a third read not one novel or short story or poem. Don't be one of those, you of the Class of 2008.

Make the love of learning central to your life. What a difference it can mean. And remember, as someone said, even the oldest book is brand-new for the reader who opens it for the first time.

You have had the great privilege of attending one of the finest colleges in the nation, where dedication to classical learning and to the arts and sciences has long been manifest. If what you have learned here makes you want to learn more, well that's the point.

Read. Read, read! Read the classics of American literature that you've never opened. Read your country's history. How can we profess to love our country and take no interest in its history? Read into the history of Greece and Rome. Read about the great turning points in the history of science and medicine and ideas.

Read for pleasure, to be sure. I adore a good thriller or a first-rate murder mystery. But take seriously—read closely—books that have stood the test of time. Study a masterpiece, take it apart, study its architecture, its vocabulary, its intent. Underline, make notes in the margins, and after a few years, go back and read it again.

Make use of the public libraries. Start your own personal library and see it grow. Talk about the books you're reading. Ask others what they're reading. You'll learn a lot.

And please, *please*, do what you can to cure the verbal virus that seems increasingly rampant among your generation. I'm talking about the relentless, wearisome use of the words "like" and "you know" and "awesome" and "actually." Listen to yourselves as you speak.

Just imagine if in his inaugural address John F. Kennedy had said, "Ask not what your country can, you know, do for you, but what you can, like, do for your country actually."

The energetic part so many of you are playing in this year's presidential race is marvelous. Keep at it, down to the wire. Keep that idealism alive. Make a difference.

Go out and get the best jobs you can and go to work with spirit. Don't get discouraged. And don't work just for money. Choose work you believe in, work you enjoy. Money enough will follow. Believe me, there's nothing like turning every day to work you love.

Walk with your heads up. And remember, honesty *is* the best policy; and yes that, too, is from Cervantes.

My warmest congratulations. In the words of the immortal Jonathan Swift, "May you live all the days of your life."

The Summons to Serve

DALLAS, TEXAS
November 22, 2013

He spoke to us in that now distant time past with a vitality and sense of purpose such as we had never heard before. He was young to be president, but it didn't seem so if you were younger still. He was ambitious to make it a better world, and so were we. "Let the word go forth [he said] . . . that the torch has been passed to a new generation of Americans."

It was an exciting time. He talked of all that needed to be done, of so much that mattered—equal opportunity, unity of purpose, education, the life of the mind and spirit, art, poetry, service to one's country, the courage to move forward into the future, the cause of peace on earth.

His was the inspiring summons to serve, to hard work and

The 50th: HONORING THE MEMORY OF
PRESIDENT JOHN F. KENNEDY

David McCullough, Dallas, November 22, 2013

worthy accomplishment, a summons we longed for. He was an optimist and he said so. But there was no sidestepping reality in what he said, no resorting to stale old platitudes.

He spoke to the point and with confidence. He knew words matter. His words changed lives. His words changed history. Rarely has a commander-in-chief addressed the nation with such command of language.

Much that he said applies now no less than half a century ago and will continue, let us hope, to be taken to heart far into the future.

"Gone but not forgotten" is the old expression for departed heroes. But if not forgotten, they are not gone.

On this day especially, and at this place, let us listen again to some of what John F. Kennedy said:

> *"The New Frontier of which I speak is not a set of promises—it is a set of challenges. It sums up not what I intend to offer the American people, but what I intend to ask of them."*
>
> *"This nation was founded by men of many nations and backgrounds. It was founded on the principle that all men are created equal, and that the rights of every man are diminished when the rights of one man are threatened. . . . The heart of the question is . . . whether we are going to treat our fellow Americans as we want to be treated."*

•   •   •

"We must educate our children as our most valuable resource. . . .

"We must have trained people—many trained people—their finest talents brought to the keenest edge. We must have not only scientists, mathematicians, and technicians. We must have people skilled in the humanities. . . .

"I look forward to an America which will reward achievement in the arts as we reward achievement in business or statecraft . . . . I look forward to an America which commands respect throughout the world not only for its strength but for its civilization."

"This country cannot afford to be materially rich and spiritually poor."

"Art is the great unifying and humanizing experience."

"The life of the arts, far from being an interruption, a distraction in the life of a nation, is very close to the center of a nation's purpose—and it is the test of the quality of a nation's civilization."

"I am certain that after the dust of centuries has passed over our cities, we, too, will be remembered not for our victories or defeats in battle or in politics, but for our contributions to the human spirit."

"If more politicians knew poetry, and more poets knew politics, I am convinced the world would be a little better place to live."

"When power leads man towards arrogance, poetry

reminds him of his limitations. When power narrows the areas of man's concern, poetry reminds him of the richness and diversity of his existence. When power corrupts, poetry cleanses, for art establishes the basic human truth which must serve as the touchstone of our judgment."

•   •   •

"Together let us explore the stars, conquer the deserts, eradicate disease, tap the ocean's depths."

"Those who came before us made certain that this country rode the first waves of the industrial revolution, the first waves of modern invention, the first waves of nuclear power, and this generation does not intend to founder in the backwash of the coming age of space. We mean to be part of it. . . . We set sail on this new sea because there is to be new knowledge to be gained, and new rights to be won, and they must be won and used for the progress of all people. . . . But why, some say, the Moon? Why choose this as our goal? . . . We choose to go to the Moon in this decade, and to do the other things, not because they are easy, but because they are hard; because that goal will serve to organize and measure the best of our energies and skills; because that challenge is one we are willing to accept, one we are unwilling to postpone, and one which we intend to win."

•   •   •

John F. Kennedy at Rice University announcing
that we will go to the Moon

"The goal of a peaceful world . . . is our guide for the present and our vision for the future . . . the quest is the greatest adventure of our century. We sometimes chafe at the burden of our obligations, the complexity of our decisions, the agony of our choices. But there is no comfort or security . . . in evasion, no solution in abdications, no relief in irresponsibility."

"The problems of the world cannot possibly be solved by skeptics or cynics, whose horizons are limited by the obvious realities. We need men who can dream of things that never were, and ask why not?"

•   •   •

"Those things that we talk about today, which seem unreal, where so many people doubt that they can be done—the fact of the matter is, it has been true all through our history—they will be done."

Again and again John Kennedy's words are fired with his love of life, his love of his country and its history. He read history, he wrote history, and he understood that history is not just about times past, but also about those who populate the present, each new generation as he liked to say, and that we, too, will be judged by history. And that we owe it to those who went before and those who will follow, to measure up, and, yes, even surpass the achievements of the past with what we accomplish and with the values we hold dear.

He also knew from his reading and from experience that very little of consequence is ever accomplished alone, but by joint effort. America has been a joint effort all down the years and we must continue in that spirit.

As he himself said, "For I can assure you that we love our country, not for what it was—though it has always been great—not for what it is—though of this we are deeply proud—but what it someday can and, through the efforts of us all, someday will be."

As his campaign song said, he had high hopes. So do we.

devotion which we bring to this endeavor will light our country and all who serve it -- and the glow from that fire can truly light the world. For "when a man's ways please the Lord, he maketh even his enemies to be at peace with him."

And so, my fellow Americans: ask not what your country will do for you -- ask what you can do for your country.

My fellow citizens of the world: ask not what America will do for you but what you can do for freedom.

Finally, whether you are citizens of America or the world, ask of me and those who serve with me the same high standards of strength and sacrifice that we will ask of you; while asking the Lord above to grant us all the strength and wisdom we shall need. With a good conscience our only sure reward, with history the final judge of our deeds, let us go

Draft of John F. Kennedy's inaugural address

A Building Like No Other

U.S. CAPITOL HISTORICAL SOCIETY
Washington, D.C.
2016

So here we are in the Capitol of the United States of America on Capitol Hill, the acropolis of our nation. It is a building like no other in the land, wherein the highest aspirations of a free and open society have been written into law, generation after generation, where, time and again, brave and eloquent words have changed history, and where the best and some of the worst of human motivations have been plainly on display.

This magnificent structure has been called "the temple of liberty" . . . "the spirit of America writ in stone" . . . "a mighty engine" . . . "an ennobling shrine" . . . "a city unto itself." Thomas Jefferson called it "the great commanding theater" of the nation. It may also be said that here on this site, within these walls, there is an abundance of story such as to be found in no other structure in our country.

Some have likened the Congress to an ever-flowing river, the content of which keeps steadily changing. From the time Congress first took up its business here on the Hill in 1800 more than eleven thousand men and women have come and gone as members of the House and Senate. The current elected members number 535. But the continuing population of this "city unto itself" is greater by far. There are a total of 1,800 Capitol Hill police serving, or a force more than three times the size of Congress. Some one hundred engineers look after the electricity, plumbing, and fire protection. Another army of workers maintains the grounds. Barbers, chefs, waiters and waitresses, a resident physician, and congressional staff members are also part of the workforce within the building.

Then there are the sixty-five tour guides who serve a steady flow of visitors numbering from three to five million a year—men, women, schoolchildren by the thousands from all parts of the country and the world.

I set foot here first as a high school student all the way from Pittsburgh. I was fifteen.

It is fitting that we do justice to the past, and that we travel far and wide to see where our history happened—to the birthplaces and homes of our notables, to Independence Hall and battlefields and legendary river crossings. But think of the volume and range and the immense consequences of so much that has taken place at this one site—the passing of the Fourteenth

Amendment, for example, or the declarations of two world wars, or approval of the Marshall Plan and building an interstate highway system like no other on earth. It was here during the Great Depression that Franklin Roosevelt said, "the only thing we have to fear is fear itself." Here, in an inaugural address known the world over, that John Kennedy called on us to "Ask not what your country can do for you—ask what you can do for your country."

To be sure, there has been no absence of pointless onstage preening in this "great commanding theater," no shortage of self-serving blather and endless days taken up with matters unbearably dull. "We have the power to do any damn fool thing we want to do, and we seem to do it about every ten minutes," one senator, William Fulbright, commented fifty years ago. And now we are confronted with the disgraceful "Dialing-for-Dollars" reality of things as they are currently in Congress.

But then history is human. History is composed of the bad and the good, as much of the goings-on here amply illustrate. There was that day on the Senate floor in 1856 when political anger turned to manic rage and a South Carolina congressman, Preston Brooks, attacking from behind with a heavy cane, tried to club to death the outspoken abolitionist Senator Charles Sumner of Massachusetts and nearly succeeded.

And there was the day in 1950 when a freshman senator from Maine, Margaret Chase Smith, had the courage to stand and challenge Senator Joseph McCarthy as no one had, saying that those who shouted loudest about Americanism all too frequently ignored such basic principles of Americanism as "the right to criticize, the right to hold unpopular beliefs, the right to protest, the right of independent thought."

Harry Truman later said to her, "Mrs. Smith, your declaration of conscience was one of the finest things that has happened here in Washington in all my years in the Senate and the White House."

As should be appreciated, too, there is here, and rightfully, an enduring pride that comes with serving one's country, of navigating with skill and to good effect within this political institution. Congresswoman Barbara Jordan once put it proudly, "I am neither a black politician nor a woman politician. Just a politician, a professional politician."

My old friend Senator Patrick Leahy of Vermont, while standing outside the Capitol on 9/11, said to himself, "Lord, let

Barbara Jordan

us get back in there . . . we had to say to the American people that we were here, including our loyal and brave staff."

Think of those who have passed through these very doors. Think of the turning points in our history that have taken place here—here where we are gathered in Statuary Hall, the old House of Representatives.

It was here that James Monroe, James Madison, John Quincy Adams, Andrew Jackson, and Millard Fillmore were all inaugurated president . . . here that a foreign citizen addressed Congress for the first time—the Marquis de Lafayette.

This is historic ground if ever there was. Congress passed the Land Grant College Act here, established the Smithsonian Institution, voted for war on Mexico, a decision strongly opposed by many, including a congressman from Illinois, Abraham Lincoln. Here, by acts of Congress, eight states became part of the Union—Alabama, Missouri, Arkansas, Michigan, Florida, Texas, Wisconsin, and California—states that in area nearly doubled the size of the country.

Acoustics in the hall were erratic, mainly terrible. From certain locations on the floor one could hear what was being said—even whispered—on the far side of the room. At the same time it was next to impossible to hear what was being said from the podium.

There are old tales of ghostly footsteps echoing here at night. According to one story, a Capitol policeman entered the hall on a New Year's Eve to find all the statues dancing.

One of the most moving moments in our country's story took place just over there. A brass plate on the floor marks the spot.

In 1831, at age sixty-three—considered quite old at the time—a newly elected member of the House, John Quincy Adams, took his seat. Thirty years earlier, in 1800, his father, President John Adams, had addressed Congress when it convened for the first time in the still unfinished Capitol. John Quincy had been an ambassador several times, a senator, secretary of state, and president. Now he had returned to the same setting where he had been inaugurated president to serve as a mere freshman congressman. It was something no president had ever done and, as he wrote in his diary, no election or appointment had ever conferred on him such pleasure— including the presidency.

He was short, portly, a bit drab in dress, not at all impressive in appearance, but he soon left little doubt as to where he stood on issues. He was determined, incorruptible. He was also one of the few members of the House whose voice could be plainly heard from the podium, acoustical problems notwithstanding. "Mr. Adams," wrote Congressman Joshua Giddings of Ohio, "belongs to no local district, no political party, but to the nation and to the people."

He loved the House of Representatives, loved the theater of all its proceedings, rarely missing even an hour when the House was in session. He worked fervently to establish the Smithsonian, opposed the war with Mexico with unfailing tenacity, and spoke with an eloquence scarcely equaled then or since—"Old Man Eloquent," he was called. He was the most

John Quincy Adams

ardent and faithful antislavery member of the House of Representatives.

Tenacity of purpose burned in him to the very end. February 21, 1848, was the day John Quincy Adams collapsed here at his desk. He died two days later. He had died "in harness," as said then.

On February 26, he lay in state here, the room packed with an immense crowd including all members of both houses, the Supreme Court, and President Andrew Jackson. "We have never witnessed a more august spectacle," wrote one Washington newspaper. "In point of character, as a man and as a politician, none of the public men at Washington," said the New York *Herald*, "are approachable to what Mr. Adams was."

Two all-important lessons of history stand clearly expressed in this our national Capitol. The first is that little of consequence is ever accomplished alone. High achievement is nearly always a joint effort, as has been shown again and again in these halls when the leaders of different parties, representatives from differing constituencies and differing points of view, have been able, for the good of the country, to put those differences aside and work together.

I witnessed this firsthand in 1978, during the Senate debate over the Panama Canal Treaty, a measure strongly favored by the Carter administration. My book on the canal, *The Path Between the Seas*, the result of six years of writing and research, had been published only the year before, and convinced as I was that the treaty was much the wisest course for our country and for Panama, I volunteered as an independent advocate for the treaty and was on hand here on the Hill through several months. At times I had the pleasure of hearing my book quoted on the Senate floor, and by those taking opposite positions. But, so it often is with history. It can serve to validate all kinds of opinions.

In the course of the debates I saw Republicans and Democrats alike change their point of view and I saw that both sides were trying to do what they felt to be the right thing. I witnessed no animosity, no enmity. In the end it was only when a number of Republicans, and Senator Howard Baker of Tennessee in particular, saw the treaty as the right course and made it a joint effort, that the treaty passed. And it has proven to have been the right decision over the past thirty-eight years.

The second lesson to be found here is that history is about far more than politics and war only. So much that is most expressive of American life and aspirations and contributions to the human spirit is to be found in the arts—in architecture, paintings, sculpture, and engineering genius. We Americans are builders at heart and in what we build we often show ourselves at our best. You have only to look around at so much to be seen in this great building.

In view of the current political climate, let me point out, too, how much of what we see throughout the building was the work of immigrants. William Thornton, a physician who won a design competition for the Capitol in 1792, was a native of Tortola in the British West Indies. Benjamin Henry Latrobe, the first professional architect to take charge of the design of the building, including this hall, was born and educated in England. James Hoban, the architect who restored the White House after it was burned by the British during the War of 1812, and who also worked on the Capitol, was from

Benjamin Latrobe by Charles Willson Peale

Ireland. And Collen Williamson, the stone mason who over-saw the laying of the foundation of the Capitol, was a Scot.

Then there was amazing Constantino Brumidi, the artist whose vibrant frescoes fill the uppermost reaches of the great Rotunda under the Capitol dome and whose decorative ge-nius brightens the corridors and hallways of the Senate wing in such a manner as rarely to be seen. A tiny figure who stood only five feet five inches tall, he was exuberant in spirit and produced work here of such monumental scale as had never been seen in our country.

There was also Carlo Franzoni, the sculptor who did the statue of Clio, the muse of history, over there, above the main door keeping note of the history taking place here.

Brumidi and Franzoni, as you might imagine, were both from Italy, as were any number of workers, skilled masons, and stonecutters.

It might also be added that our capital city, Washington, was itself the design of an immigrant, the French engineer

Constantino Brumidi

Pierre L'Enfant, and that the two finest, most famous movies ever made about Congress, *Mr. Smith Goes to Washington* and *Advise and Consent*, were directed by immigrants, Frank Capra and Otto Preminger, respectively.

And yes, there were the African American slaves who did much of the work on the Capitol—how many in all will never be known, but play a large part they did. Notable evidence of their labors are the pillars that stand all about us here. "Hired out" by their owners, they cut the marble in the quarries.

Building and rebuilding the Capitol took more time and labor and patience than many might imagine. Things went wrong. There were angry differences of opinion over matters of all kinds. There were accidents, numerous injuries, and one dramatic, narrow escape.

At work one day on his frescoes in the upper reaches of the great dome, Brumidi slipped from his scaffold and only just managed to catch hold of a rung of the ladder and for fifteen minutes hung for dear life with both hands some fifty-five feet above the marble floor until a Capitol policeman happened to glance up and rushed to the rescue. Brumidi by then was seventy-two and had been at work in the Capitol for twenty-six years.

The great dome famously took form through the Civil War and remains as intended the colossal commanding focal point of our capital city. It is primarily the work of two exceptional Americans, architect Thomas U. Walter and structural engineer Montgomery C. Meigs, each a story. Walter started out as a bricklayer. Meigs, a captain in the Army Corps of Engineers, was all of thirty-six when he took on one of the most challenging engineering assignments ever and created what stands as a masterpiece of nineteenth-century engineering with inner and outer cast-iron shells weighing nearly nine million pounds.

A great lover of the arts and an artist himself, Meigs also had much to do with the art that was to fill the building—including the part played by Brumidi and the choice of the American sculptor Thomas Crawford to create the nineteen-and-a-half-

U.S. Capitol under construction

The Statue of Freedom, U.S. Capitol

foot-high Statue of Freedom that would stand atop the dome.

Completed in 1868, the gleaming dome remains the focal point of our capital city and though there have been modifications and additions to the building in the years since, it remains essentially as it was then, a symbol of freedom, the structure bespeaking more than any other our history, our American journey, evoking and encouraging powerfully pride in our system and, yes, patriotism.

And now we are in the midst of another election season, which like so many before will determine much to follow— more than we can possibly know.

Over there above the door, on the side of Clio's chariot, is the work of the Massachusetts clockmaker Simon Willard. It has been doing its job a long time, since 1837, one hundred and seventy-nine years ago. It ticks on, still keeping perfect time.

My feeling is Clio, too, is attending to her role now no less than ever, taking note of the history we are and will be making.

On we go.

Acknowledgments

Again I am gratefully indebted to those of my family, friends, and working associates who helped make this book possible: my daughter Dorie Lawson, who over the years made all the arrangements for the speeches I've given and who assembled and sorted them and helped select those that seemed most applicable to the present moment in our country; then there was the part played in this same process by my son Geoffrey, Melissa Marchetti, and my gifted research assistant of long standing, Mike Hill; my editor, Bob Bender, whose close reading and suggestions have been, once again, of great help; my literary agent, Morton Janklow, particularly for his immediate enthusiasm for the idea; to all of my family including those grandchildren to whom the book is dedicated, and, above all, as always, to my editor-in-chief, my wife, Rosalee.

Photo Credits

Page 2:   U.S. Senate Historical Office

Page 4:   National Gallery of Art

Page 7:   Library of Congress

Page 13:   Courtesy of Architect of the Capitol/U.S. Capitol Historical Society

Page 18:   University of Pittsburgh

Page 26:   © Thomas Jefferson Foundation at Monticello

Page 30:   Courtesy of Harry S. Truman Library & Museum

Page 35:   Courtesy of Union College

Page 36:   Courtesy of Union College

Page 44:   "John Dickinson by Charles Willson Peale, from life, 1782–1783," courtesy of Independence National Historical Park

Page 45:   "Benjamin Rush by Charles Willson Peale, after Thomas Sully, 1818," courtesy of Independence National Historical Park

Page 56:   National Gallery of Art

Page 66:   Courtesy of Theodore Roosevelt Collection, Harvard College Library

Page 70:   The Ronald Reagan Library

Page 71:   Franklin D. Roosevelt Presidential Library & Museum

Page 74:   Bradley Smith, Courtesy of Harry S. Truman Library & Museum

PHOTO CREDITS

Page 81: White House Collection/White House Historical Association

Page 84: Courtesy of The Carpenters' Company, Philadelphia, PA

Page 88: National Gallery of Art

Page 96: Courtesy of Ohio University

Page 110: Courtesy of the Yale University Art Gallery

Page 122: Portrait of the Marquis de Lafayette by Samuel F. B. Morse, 1826, oil on canvas. Photograph by Glenn Castellano, Collection of the Public Design Commission of the City of New York

Page 126: AFP/Getty Images

Page 131: Library of Congress

Page 133: Library of Congress

Page 137: National Park Service, U.S. Department of the Interior

Page 144: Library of Congress

Page 146: Real Academia de la Historia, Madrid, Spain/Bridgeman Images

Page 150: Tom Fox, © 2013, The Dallas Morning News

Page 154: Photo 12/Universal Images Group/Getty Images

Page 156: Tom Williams/National Archives/Getty Images

Page 160: LBJ Library, photo by Frank Wolfe

Page 163: © The Metropolitan Museum of Art/Art Resource, NY

Page 166: Private Collection, Peter Newark Pictures/Bridgeman Images

Page 167: Library of Congress

Page 169: Courtesy of Architect of the Capitol

Page 170: Bruce Guthrie, photo credit

Frontispiece: Collection of the Massachusetts Historical Society

Also by
DAVID McCULLOUGH

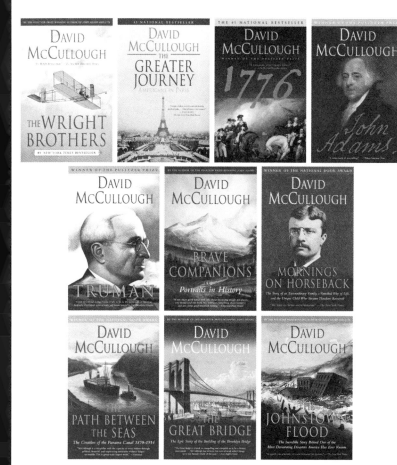

Pick up or download your copies today!

50209